COMMUNITY-ENGAGED RESEARCH FOR RESILIENCE AND HEALTH

Interdisciplinary Community-Engaged Research for Health Series

The *Interdisciplinary Community-Engaged Research for Health* series aims to bridge the gap between researchers and practitioners to facilitate the development of collaborative, equitable research and action. The reality of persistent health disparities and structural inequalities highlights the need for new strategies that are social justice–driven. Traditionally, efforts have tended to be institution-based, "expert"-focused, and silo-specific. To promote health equity, diverse stakeholders with different types of expertise need to work together to solve real-world problems. This series publishes books that recognize the importance of diverse collaboration and equip readers from a variety of backgrounds with the tools and vision to center community voice in research for action.

Series Editors

Farrah Jacquez
University of Cincinnati

Lina Svedin
University of Utah

Advisory Board

Sherrie Flynt Wallington
George Washington University

Jennifer Malat
University of Cincinnati

Kristin Kalsem
University of Cincinnati

Kathleen Thiede Call
University of Minnesota

Andriana Abariotes
University of Minnesota

COMMUNITY-ENGAGED RESEARCH FOR RESILIENCE AND HEALTH

Interdisciplinary Community-Engaged Research for Health Series

Volume 4

Edited by Kelli E. Canada & Clark M. Peters

About the University of Cincinnati Press
The University of Cincinnati Press is committed to publishing rigorous, peer-reviewed, leading scholarship accessibly to stimulate dialog among the academy, public intellectuals, and lay practitioners. The Press endeavors to erase disciplinary boundaries in order to cast fresh light on common problems in our global community. Building on the university's long-standing tradition of social responsibility to the citizens of Cincinnati, state of Ohio, and the world, the Press publishes books on topics that expose and resolve disparities at every level of society and have local, national, and global impact.

The University of Cincinnati Press, Cincinnati 45221
Copyright © 2022

All rights reserved. No part of this book may be reproduced or utilized in any form or by any means, electronic or mechanical, or by any information storage and retrieval system, without written permission from the publisher. Requests for permission to reproduce material from this work should be sent to University of Cincinnati Press, Langsam Library, 2911 Woodside Drive, Cincinnati, Ohio 45221
ucincinnatipress.uc.edu

ISBN 978-1-947602-81-6 (paperback)
ISBN 978-1-947602-82-3 (e-book, PDF)
ISBN 978-1-947602-83-0 (e-book, EPUB)

Library of Congress Cataloging-in-Publication Data

Names: Canada, Kelli E., editor. | Peters, Clark M., editor.
Title: Community-engaged research for resilience and health / edited by
   Kelli E. Canada & Clark M. Peters.
Description: Cincinnati : University of Cincinnati Press, [2022] | Series:
   Interdisciplinary community-engaged research for health series ; volume 4
   | Includes bibliographical references and index. | Summary: "This volume is centered on how
   interdisciplinary scholar-practitioner teams are working to promote resilience in communities
   facing health crises and/or in underserved populations. The focus on resilience seeks to highlight
   what works and lift up those programs and interventions that make a difference in communities
   grappling with social determinants of health, such as addiction, domestic violence, poverty,
   or discrimination. Editors Kelli Canada and Clark Peters argue that a dual approach, research
   and action dedicated to increasing internal communal support while simultaneously working
   to break down barriers to health. The chapter authors in this volume show that researching
   and highlighting community based solutions, points of strength, and sources of resilience
   help communities survive and thrive in the face of adversity"-- Provided by publisher.
Identifiers: LCCN 2022004997 (print) | LCCN 2022004998 (ebook) | ISBN
   9781947602816 (paperback) | ISBN 9781947602823 (pdf) | ISBN 9781947602830 (epub)
Subjects: LCSH: Public health--Social aspects. | Social medicine. | Community health services.
Classification: LCC RA418 .C6694 2022 (print) | LCC RA418 (ebook) | DDC
   362.1--dc23/eng/20220218
LC record available at https://lccn.loc.gov/2022004997
LC ebook record available at https://lccn.loc.gov/2022004998

Designed and produced for UC Press by Jennifer Flint
Typeset in Granjon LT Std
Printed in the United States of America
First Printing

Contents

1. Community Engagement in the Study of Resilience — 1
   Kelli E. Canada and Clark M. Peters

2. The Black Girls Advocacy and Leadership Alliance: Community-Based Participatory Research (CBPR) to Advance Equity and Collective Resilience for Black Girls — 15
   Sara Goodkind, Britney G. Brinkman, and Kathi Elliott

3. Insights from Project Youth MIND: Building a Virtual Youth Community during a Health and Racial Pandemic — 41
   Michelle C. Chatman and Ryan T. Wright

4. Shifting the Lens from Traditional Medical Research to Fostering Community Resilience — 75
   Quianta Moore

5. The Resilience Dilemma — 103
   Jomo Kheru

6. The Gift of Resilience Among Youths from Oakland — 131
   Regina Jackson

7. Promoting Resilience Through Community-Engaged Research with a Community-Based Clinician — 155
   Rachel Jones

8. Researching Resilience: Collaboration and Critique Through Community Engagement — 183
   Clark M. Peters and Kelli E. Canada

Bios 199

Index 203

COMMUNITY-ENGAGED RESEARCH FOR RESILIENCE AND HEALTH

Chapter 1

Community Engagement in the Study of Resilience

Kelli E. Canada and Clark M. Peters

> *Resilience as an ecological construct suggests that more than individual capacity is necessary to positively adapt under adversity, but positive development relies heavily on context, access to resources, and cultural relevance and meaning*
> Anderson, 2019, p. 7

As the body of resilience research expands, theories of resilience and how the construct is understood at the individual and community levels continue to evolve (Fleming & Ledogar, 2008). Once thought to be a singular trait of an individual who faced serious adversity but was able to positively adapt (Luthar, 2000), it is now conceptualized as a construct deeply embedded within the multiple systems people and communities navigate (Anderson, 2019; Shaw et al., 2016). Conducting research in collaboration with communities is a critical element of understanding how multiple, intertwined systems create, disrupt, and impede resilience and, more broadly, responses to adversity, trauma, and oppression. Research surrounding resilience is especially vulnerable to misrepresentation when a community of people, actions or inactions, and behavioral responses are misperceived by researchers. Although there is a spectrum of research approaches that involves community engagement, one prominent model is community-based participatory research (CBPR). Methods drawn from this model demonstrate the potential to increase the accuracy of research, facilitate opportunities for the co-construction of knowledge, and create more equity across the research process.

This book both celebrates and interrogates the concept of resilience. We do this through breaking the concept away from traditional views of individual resilience and reconstructing it to hinge on the community of context. This volume highlights six projects that utilize CBPR strategies to build knowledge and create action within vulnerable and resilient communities around the United States. These projects highlight the many ways to study resilience within research projects and build resilience among research participants and communities. Chapter authors also reflect on how they experience their own resilience through CBPR engagement. Each chapter brings a different focus; some chapters discuss the research process and findings, while others offer a reflection of the authors' experiences working within CBPR. Chapter authors may offer alternative definitions of resilience and how these definitions blossomed through their community-engaged research practices. Chapters are woven together, however, with their celebration and critique of the concept of resilience and traditional research approaches involving marginalized communities. Authors offer alternative frameworks to resilience and suggest ways of using CBPR to address the shortcomings of the concept. Given the diversity in perspective, this book is intended for researchers of all kinds, from the professional to the practical, including community members exploring how best to reach their goals, students seeking to understand how to conduct effective and meaningful research, partners in philanthropy and state and local government, and academics looking to impact and inform audiences outside the academy.

Chapter authors from this volume are alumni of a leadership training project funded through the Robert Wood Johnson Foundation called Interdisciplinary Research Leaders (IRL). The purpose of IRL was to bring researchers and community members together to learn the strategies needed to successfully carry out CBPR and build leadership skills to promote a *culture of health*. A culture of health signifies that all people and communities have an equal opportunity to thrive and flourish; this means that all communities are equitable and have access to healthy and fresh foods, quality and integrated healthcare services, safe and affordable housing, economic mobility, and social supports (Robert Wood Johnson Foundation, 2021). The specific steps and strategies that must be taken to build a culture of health within communities will look different by place and cultural context. As communities examine their own strengths and resources, building on existing community resilience to challenge and dismantle racism and oppression is a critical first step in constructing a culture of health where community strengths and resources will flourish. Chapter authors received a competitive grant to develop leadership skills and use CBPR as a vehicle to engage communities in the research process, examine avenues of resilience, and begin working to build a culture of health.

In this first chapter, key concepts are defined. The concept of resilience within traditional approaches to research are explored and contrasted with approaches used in CBPR. Research on resilience is also examined within vulnerable, marginalized, or oppressed communities. Although CBPR approaches are largely celebrated as an essential method when working within resilience-related research, the limitations and challenges inherent in CBPR are noted along with alternative approaches to use across the community-engaged research continuum. This chapter ends with a summary of the six projects highlighted in this volume.

Community-Based Participatory Research and the Study of Resilience

CBPR is a necessary strategy to accurately research resilience. Research, for many disciplines, does not historically include participation from members of the community beyond being subjects in the research project. This exclusion leads to both translational and implementation challenges, but also increases the risk of harm to marginalized, under-represented, and historically oppressed communities. Community-engaged research falls along a continuum ranging from community-based (i.e., research takes place in the community rather than a lab) to community-driven (i.e., active participation by community in the research process; Hacker, 2013). Researchers use a variety of terms when describing community-engaged research. In their review of CBPR with youth, Jacquez and colleagues (2013) found that CBPR terminology varied by discipline. It was described as "action research," "community-engaged research," or simply "participatory research," in addition to CBPR. Research described as CBPR also varied from community stakeholders being involved only minimally in research question development to more extensive collaborations involving community participation at each phase of the research.

CBPR traditionally involves active participation from the community in every phase of the research through a collaborative partnership with the research team. In other words, in CBPR, community members work closely with the research team to identify the problem, develop the research questions and methods, collect data, conduct the data analysis, interpret results, and disseminate findings (Hacker, 2013). In CBPR, data are shared and knowledge is co-created by the researchers and community. Hacker (2013) outlined nine central principles of CBPR work, which include:

1. Define "community"—who is in "the community"
2. Work with community to identify and build on the strengths and resources in the community—what does the community perceive they do well; what do they perceive as their greatest resources
3. Facilitate collaborative, equitable partnerships throughout all phases of the research and create specific power-sharing processes
4. Create opportunities for co-learning and capacity building for both academics and community members
5. Balance knowledge generation and intervention as dual goals in the research
6. Focus on the *local* relevance of public health problems and *local* determinants of health
7. Create new and modified systems of communication and knowledge sharing using iterative processes (e.g., working back and forth until the system is mutually beneficial)
8. Create strategies to disseminate results widely to all participants in the CBPR project and for all participants to then disseminate results to a broader audience
9. Commit from the beginning of the work to identify opportunities for sustainable practices

Community-engaged work—particularly CBPR—is rooted in social justice and is intended to flatten the power imbalance that researchers often contend with, where knowledge is owned by academia and communities are used as laboratories. "Communities" may be individual groups of people with a common demographic or problem area, neighborhoods within a set geographic region, or a group of people with a shared culture, for example. This history of using communities for data access intersects both racism and oppression. Many communities never benefit from the research they participated in and historically, far too many people were harmed in the research process. CBPR is one strategy to create space for community empowerment through collaborative research. This collaborative process integrates community stakeholders' perceptions and researcher expertise to identify research priorities. Although it does not erase the history of trauma and abuse at the hands of researchers, CBPR does have the potential to create a different path for the co-creation of knowledge.

This co-creation of knowledge is essential when studying culturally- and structurally-bound concepts like resilience. Resilience is broadly defined as "good outcomes in spite of serious threats to adaptation or development" (Masten, 2001, p. 228). The concept of resilience grew out of a strengths-based model and as a rejoinder to approaches solely focusing on deficits. Resilience is more fluid than static; people and communities may have more or less resilience over time. Resilience can be an individual trait, but also embodies characteristics that span familial, social, cultural, and political systems. Acknowledging the complex systems that individuals and communities are nestled within is critical in the study of resilience. Anderson (2019) argued that "For African American families who suffer from macro-level stressors and chronic adversity, and have done so for generations, applying simplistic ways of knowing and understanding to their processes of resilience is simply inadequate" (p. 7). The study of resilience—from conceptualization to measurement—rests on a foundation of collaborative, community-engaged approaches to research. When normative definitions of resilience are applied in research without community and cultural context, the term may lose meaning and, in some cases, cause real harm through placing blame on individuals.

Resilience research is often conceptualized as a response to risk exposure. "Risk," however, is ambiguous and varies in definition depending on who is defining it. The very definition of risk is best developed using a constructivist lens—that is, working from a local perspective to conceptualize and determine best strategies for defining and measuring risk (Hutcheon & Lashewicz, 2014). The general literature on risk tends to focus on events that are more acute or imminent in nature rather than conceptualizing risk as the result of chronic exposure to adversity. Resilience building and risk prevention programs and policies that are formed without understanding the population to be served or are not inclusive of the population's perspective may rely on normative or dominant culture definitions of risk and resilience (Howard, Dryden, & Johnson, 2010). Allen and colleagues (2014) suggested that "Understanding how 'unusual' behavior patterns may be locally functional in a distinctively configured cultural ecology, when alternative and more conventional pathways to development are blocked, may be critical to understanding resilience" (p. 605). These researchers worked across five sites with Indigenous communities. Each site was unique in how community members exhibited community resilience through networks of people, innovations, ritual, story-telling, and restorative practices.

CBPR approaches are necessary to identify the nuances of resilience across and within communities. Jumper-Reeves and colleagues (2014) argued that traditional models of research on the effectiveness of resilience-building interventions for Indigenous communities is inherently flawed. Without community voice, Western culture dominates research paradigms, which dismisses important contextual factors that are central for building resilience in certain ethnic and racial groups. Jumper-Reeves and colleagues suggest that CBPR allows for the assessment of how well the intervention resonates or aligns with cultural norms and customs—a critical component for successful implementation and intervention effectiveness.

Working with communities through CBPR reveals both the complexities and commonalities of concepts like resilience. Although we often think of access to services as a key source of resilience, through CBPR, Shetgriri and colleagues (2009) highlighted the importance of the family unit over community-based services in the Latinx community they researched. Families within this community perceived that successfully engaging with young people stemmed from the family unit rather than available community resources. Resilience-building programs for this community required avenues for participation from parents and other key members of the family unit in addition to the youths (Shetgiri et al., 2009). In related resilience and CBPR projects, teams worked with youths to build resilience within an immigrant community through youth empowerment (Ferrera et al., 2015). Teams developed steering committees of community, adolescents, family, and elders as experts in order to raise awareness about the historical meaning of the problems they were challenged to change (Jumper-Reeves et al., 2014). They collected data from community members and presented these data back to the larger community to identify the results that resonated with the community at large as one step in the development of culturally- and ethically-responsive interventions to promote family-level resilience among low-income families (Woods-Jaeger et al., 2018). These CBPR strategies not only speed the uptake of research in communities, they also work to make research an accessible and relevant tool for communities to address local problems and achieve shared goals (Hacker, 2013).

CBPR in Action

In this volume, the authors—six researchers and their community partners—document their CBPR journeys to advance a culture of health in their own respective ways. The authors describe their paths into this interdisciplinary work, how they entered the CBPR space, and the resources and challenges they met along the way. In addition, the authors interrogate the concept of resilience and position it within the CBPR framework. They also reflect on their experiences, lessons learned, and next steps in future work. In Chapter 2, Sara Goodkind, Britney G. Brinkman, and Kathi Elliott describe their long-standing partnership centered on the Black Girls Advocacy and Leadership Alliance (BGALA). They argue that relationships and trust are central to CBPR. These kinds of partnerships require all members to be authentic, slow down, be flexible, and engage in work that is community driven (as opposed to solely research driven). This academic–community partnership is strengthened by the active participation of Black girls in the community, government leaders, and other community-based organizations. The authors highlight key lessons they learned and offer guidance to people who are interested in forming these partnerships.

In Chapter 3, we head to Washington, D.C., where Michelle Chatman and Ryan Wright describe Project Youth MIND and reflect on "doing and teaching mindfulness" to promote resilience. The authors document their personal journeys, as well as how they integrated their journeys into research and practice with Black urban youths through the use of a culturally responsive approach to support personal resilience building. They reflect on Project Youth MIND and the lessons learned in this research as it intersected with the COVID-19 pandemic. In addition, the authors describe the twists and turns of their project and how Black urban youths embraced the principles and practices underlying mindfulness. They embrace the contexts that presented themselves so vividly in their work—the impacts of COVID-19 and Black Lives Matter movement.

Dr. Quianta Moore describes her process in CBPR and the dire need for this approach to research in the medical field in Chapter 4. Her chapter, "Shifting the Lens from Traditional Medical Research to Fostering Community Resilience," examines the interconnectedness of individual and community resilience, and presents an overview of the different ways that resilience can be conceptualized. She emphasizes the important role that access to resources plays in resilience but challenges the research enterprise whereby advances in medicine are not always accessible to the most vulnerable members of the U.S. In fact, the historical abuse of people of color for research purposes is juxtaposed with the stark realities that these very communities often lack access to high-quality medical care that was developed through research. Moore presents a case study using CBPR in medical research and suggests that this approach is a strong example of how decentralizing power in research can actually work to heal communities.

In "The Resilience Dilemma," (Chapter 5), Jomo Kheru investigates the complexities of the term "resilience." Deploying an African-centered lens, he explores the concept, identifying the racial trauma embedded in the education system and other contexts our youths live within. Kheru offers specific recommendations regarding healthy boundaries and safe limitations in community-engaged research with historically marginalized populations. For all research, especially that which is centered on Black populations, he advocates for research team members to be proficient in African culture and Black psychology. He discusses the utility and power in the structured dialogue method, which is a culturally responsive communication platform that creates space to build community and *lean into* disagreement while encouraging "solidarity, trust, and conviction."

In Chapter 6, Regina Jackson, a community leader in Oakland, California, reflects on her CBPR journey. She relates the experience of engaging in CBPR from a community member's perspective. As the leader of an organization that works with youths in Oakland, she describes the immense responsibility she felt to vet researchers fully before she agreed to let them work with her, her colleagues, and youths. Jackson prioritized feelings of trust, time spent in the agency, shared values with the researchers, and a shared focus on research priorities as the key factors in decisions around engaging in CBPR. She felt protective of the youths in her organization and wanted to enforce safeguards to ensure that her children would truly benefit from the research and not be harmed. In her chapter, Jackson walks us through how community resilience can actually grow through CBPR work.

Finally, in Chapter 7, Rachel Jones provides a reflection and roadmap for community providers who are interested in research collaboration. She presents considerations, types of collaboration, and practical input (e.g., time allocation, logistics, boundary setting) in the chapter. Jones, a licensed practicing counselor, describes the clinical work she did with families to help them build individual and family resilience throughout her career. She highlights the body of work that defines resilience and thriving in clinical and personal practice. The ability to bounce back from adversity is one that she had to call upon both personally and professionally on her CBPR path. Jones argues that communication between community partners and researchers is critically important, especially when working with mental health and medical practitioners. In these cases, research cannot always take priority, especially when lives are at stake. Jones weaves in a narrative of how she built her own personal resilience when faced with life and professional trauma.

Conclusion

This volume offers an in-depth look at CBPR projects in action—a perspective that is often lost in traditional academic writing. These projects, as well as many others, emphasize the value, uniqueness, and depth that emerge from collaborative, participatory work with communities. Across chapters, the authors describe the ways CBPR can improve the research process and ethical strategies for engaging vulnerable communities in research. The authors also share specific examples of how they started their CBPR work, generated research questions collaboratively, and worked collectively to develop culturally-informed practices for data collection. Themes surrounding the effective dissemination of findings to various stakeholders and through major political and public health-related crises are documented across chapters. The authors in this collection also grapple with the concept of resilience and identify the controversies surrounding the use of this concept while also recognizing its value when locally defined to capture personal and community strength. The co-creation of knowledge is a necessary step in developing interventions to build a sustainable culture of health for all people. Interpreting the meaning of patterns identified in research on resilience and using this to create interventions is best understood through a CBPR process. As James Charlton (1998) wrote in his book on disability rights and oppression, "Nothing about us without us." This idea of community inclusion is especially true in research endeavors and, like many authors illustrate in this volume, actually creates the opportunity for research to be more translational and impactful for the communities they are intended to serve. Whether interested in CBPR or curious about the ways these projects unfold, the chapters in this volume bring perspective to seasoned researchers, students, and community practitioners alike.

References

Allen, J., Hopper, K., Wexler, L., Kral, M., Rasmus, S., & Nystad, K. (2014). Mapping resilience pathways of Indigenous youth in five circumpolar communities. *Transcultural Psychiatry*, *51*(5), 601–631. https://doi.org/10.1177/1363461513497232

Anderson, L. (2019). Rethinking resilience theory in African American families: Fostering positive adaptations and transformative social justice. *Journal of Family Theory & Review*, 1–13. https://doi.org/10.1111/jftr.12343

Charlton, J. I. (1998). *Nothing about us without us: Disability oppression and empowerment*. University of California Press.

Ferrera, M. J., Sacks, T. K., Perez, M., Nixon, J. P., Asis, D., & Coleman, W. L. (2015). Empowering immigrant youth in Chicago. *Family Community Health*, *38*(1), 12–21. https://doi.org/10.1097/FCH.0000000000000058

Fleming, J. & Ledogar, R. J. (2008). Resilience, an evolving concept: A review of the literature relevant to Aboriginal research. *Pimatisiwin*, *6*(2), 7–23.

Hacker, K. (2013). *Community-based participatory research*. Sage.

Howard, S., Dryden, J., & Johnson, B. (2009). Childhood resilience: Review and critique of literature. *Oxford Review of Education*, *25*(3), 307–323. https://doi.org/10.1080/030549899104008

Hutcheon, E. & Lashewicz, B. (2014). Theorizing resilience: Critiquing and unbounding a marginalizing concept, *Disability & Society*, *29*(9), 1383–1397. https://doi.org/10.1080/09687599.2014.934954

Jacquez, F., Vaughn, L. M., & Wagner, E. (2013). Youth as partners, participants, or passive recipients: A review of children and adolescents in community-based participatory research (CBPR). *American Journal of Psychology*, *51*, 176–189. https://doi.org/10.1007/s10464-012-9533-7

Jumper-Reeves, L., Dustman, P. A., Harthun, M. L., Kulis, S., & Brown, E. F. (2014). American Indian cultures: How CBPR illuminated intertribal cultural elements fundamental to an adaptation effort. *Prevention Science*, *15*, 547–556. https://doi.org/10.1007/s11121-012-0361-7

Luthar, S. S. (2000). The construct of resilience: A critical evaluation and guidelines for future work. *Child Development*, *71*(3), 543–562.

Masten, A. S. (2001). Ordinary magic: Resilience processes in development. *American Psychologist*, *56*(3), 227–238. https://doi.org/10.1037//0003-066X.56.3.227

Robert Wood Johnson Foundation. (2021). *About a culture of health*. From https://www.rwjf.org/en/cultureofhealth/about.html

Shaw, J., McLean, K. C., Taylor, B., Swartout, K., & Querna, K. (2016). Beyond resilience: Why we need to look at systems too. *Psychology of Violence, 6*(1), 34–41.

Shetgiri, R., Kataoka, S. H., Ryan, G. W., Askew, L. M., Chung, P. J., & Schuster, M. A. (2009). Risk and resilience in Latinos: A community-based participatory research study. *American Journal of Preventive Medicine, 37*(6), S217–S224. https://doi.org/10.1016/j.amepre.2009.08.001

Woods-Jaeger, B. A., Cho, B., Sexton, C. C., Slagel, L., & Goggin, K. (2018). Promoting resilience: Breaking the intergenerational cycle of adverse childhood experiences. *Health Education & Behavior, 45*(5), 772–780. https://doi.org/10.1177/1090198117752785

Chapter 2

The Black Girls Advocacy and Leadership Alliance

Community-Based Participatory Research (CBPR)
to Advance Equity and Collective Resilience for Black Girls

Sara Goodkind, Britney G. Brinkman, and Kathi Elliott

This chapter describes reflections on a community-based participatory research (CBPR) project focused on the Black Girls Advocacy and Leadership Alliance (BGALA), an empowerment program designed to promote collective resilience among Black girls through their involvement in critical reflection and systemic change. Supported by the Robert Wood Johnson Foundation's Interdisciplinary Research Leaders program, BGALA was collaboratively designed by an interdisciplinary group of academics and a community agency working with Black girls as a means to incorporate those girls into the broader advocacy efforts of the Black Girls Equity Alliance (BGEA). The BGEA, founded in Allegheny County, Pennsylvania, in 2017, is focused on eradicating systemic inequities affecting Black girls in our region and is comprised of individuals, community-based organizations, universities, and government entities. This chapter presents the histories of BGEA and BGALA, and lessons learned from our participatory research and collaborative advocacy.

Introduction

Black girls in the U.S. experience a double bind. Experiences of oppression—and the stress of working to overcome oppressive circumstances—can be harmful to their health. Thus, we should not expect Black girls to be individually resilient in the face of structural inequities. However, when they resist oppression, Black girls are often labeled "defiant" or "delinquent" and may experience disciplinary consequences, including justice system involvement (Morris, 2016). Empowerment programming presents a potential means for Black girls to escape this double bind by channeling their justified resistance to oppression into collective action to address societal inequities, and thus, helping to develop their collective resilience. In this chapter, we describe the development and evaluation of an empowerment program for Black girls that emerged from a community–academic partnership between Gwen's Girls, Inc., an agency dedicated to providing gender- and culturally-responsive programming and support for Black girls, and researchers from both the University of Pittsburgh and Point Park University. We review the broader community context, including the development of the Black Girls Equity Alliance (BGEA), a collaborative alliance advocating for equity for Black girls, and highlight lessons learned about community-engaged research and resilience.

Background: The Black Girls Equity Alliance (BGEA)

In 2016, leaders of two local philanthropic foundations in the greater Pittsburgh metropolitan area convened a group of child welfare system leaders, service providers, advocates, and academics to share what they knew about inequities affecting Black girls in the region. They invited local professionals working in specific areas to bring a summary of data from their areas of expertise, such that the meeting included two people from the Allegheny County Department of Human Services sharing data on girls' child welfare involvement; attorneys from two local advocacy organizations—one focused on women and girls and one on education—providing data on Title IX and school pushout; two leaders of agencies engaged in advocacy with and service provision for Black girls contributing insight and data from their work with girls; and two academics—one presenting data on girls' health and health behaviors and the other on girls' justice system involvement. The goal was to bring together data and actors from various sites to gain a comprehensive understanding of the systemic inequities affecting Black girls in our region and to begin a collective conversation about how to address them.

This initial meeting was motivated by national calls (by Michelle Obama, Kimberlé Crenshaw, and others) to focus attention and resources on Black girls, who are often missed in conversations on gender equity that center on White girls and in conversations on racial equity that focus on Black boys. In other words, Black girls have unique experiences of marginalization that racial and gender frameworks often miss when these forms of oppression are examined separately (Crenshaw, Ocen, & Nanda, 2015). For the initial convening, one of us (Sara) calculated rates of racial disproportionality in referrals of young people to the juvenile justice system in Allegheny County, which revealed that the magnitude of racial difference is much larger in our county than in the nation. At that time, in Allegheny County, Pennsylvania, which includes the city of Pittsburgh, Black girls were eleven times more likely than White girls to be referred to the juvenile justice system (currently it is ten times), while nationally, Black girls are referred three times as often as White girls (Allegheny County Health Department et al., 2014; Allegheny

County JPO, 2020; Goodkind, 2016; Puzzanchera, Sladky, & Kang, 2019; Sickmund, Sladky, & Kang, 2020). These differential rates *cannot* be explained by differences in behaviors for which young people can be referred to juvenile justice, which we recognized when we compared the self-report and justice system data that this meeting prompted us to examine in tandem (Goodkind, 2016).

Through this initial conversation, we collectively determined that to address these inequities, we needed to develop a sense of urgency among policymakers and system actors. We believed a good way to do so would be to share these data with the broader public. Thus, we produced a collaborative report entitled *Inequities Affecting Black Girls in Pittsburgh and Allegheny County* (Goodkind, 2016). Key findings of this report included the following: In Pittsburgh, 55% of Black girls were living in poverty, compared to 15% of White girls. Black girls in Allegheny County were four times more likely than White girls to be referred to the child welfare system, to be investigated by child welfare, to have their cases accepted for service by the child welfare system, and to be removed from their homes. As noted, Black girls in Allegheny County were referred to the juvenile justice system at a rate eleven times higher than that of White girls. Further, Black girls in Allegheny County were less likely to benefit from diversion programs, with only 40% of Black girls referred to juvenile justice diverted from formal processing in the juvenile justice system, compared to 47% of White girls. In sum, we documented that Black girls were experiencing numerous, interrelated systemic inequities that could not be adequately addressed by supporting individual girls but rather, necessitated structural, systemic change.

We presented findings from this report at the first annual Equity Summit sponsored by the Gwendolyn J. Elliott Institute (GJEI), the research and training arm of Kathi's organization Gwen's Girls, an agency dedicated to providing programming and advocacy for Black girls in our county. (Britney and Sara have been members of GJEI since its inception, and were invited to join by the previous executive director of Gwen's Girls.) This summit, which over 200 people attended, and the disturbing findings of the report served as a call to action. Following the summit, Kathi and the GJEI organized a reconvening of all those interested in addressing the inequities documented in the report. As we began to meet regularly and organize ourselves into workgroups to focus on addressing the specific issues raised, we discovered that we needed to name our growing collective. Lively conversations ensued in each of the four workgroups: education, child welfare, juvenile justice, and health & wellness. One important question that provoked much conversation was, should our name include "Black" as well as "girls" since our advocacy efforts were focused on Black girls? Some members were concerned that specifying our focus on *Black* girls might limit interest or involvement, but through extensive discussion we agreed that we would name our intentions, while emphasizing that changing our systems to better support those most marginalized will ultimately make them better for all young people.

We draw from our recent report on the formation of the Black Girls Equity Alliance (BGEA) to articulate its structure and values (Brinkman et al., 2019), which we produced to share our process with people in other localities, given that Kathi has been receiving many inquiries from those who would like to form similar initiatives. BGEA works as an interprofessional alliance seeking to inform providers, communities, and systems about best practices for supporting Black girls and advocating for policy changes that will improve their lives. Individual and organizational members work collaboratively, sharing resources and decision-making power. BGEA has created a space for collaborative interdisciplinary initiatives, data-driven problem solving, participatory action research, and the honing of community resources to better serve the needs of Black girls across institutions in the realms of health and wellness, education, juvenile justice, and child welfare. The BGEA is interdisciplinary, with members from a range of backgrounds, training, and credentials, and we work toward common goals with specific shared values, including the following:

1. *Center the voices of Black girls.* "Nothing about us, without us," a phrase borrowed from the disability justice movement in the U.S., is a guiding principle of all our work. We integrate the expertise, voices, and lived experiences of Black girls throughout our work. Black girls' perspectives inform the research projects we undertake, the areas of advocacy we pursue, and the strategies for change we engage. In addition, Black girls are directly involved in all of the activities of BGEA.
2. *Emphasize structural changes.* We believe that adults are integral to undoing the gendered racism within systems—which disproportionally impacts Black girls—and we should not expect Black girls to be "resilient" in the face of structural inequities. Data about the discrepancies in outcomes for Black girls must be understood within a framework of equity that addresses the systemic barriers that lead to inequities in individual girls' experiences.
3. *Apply an intersectionality framework.* Our work with Black girls is situated within an intersectionality framework, building upon the work of Black feminist scholars and activists, including Kimberlé Crenshaw, Patricia Hill Collins, and others. Intersectionality theory provides a framework for exploring how Black girls' multiple social identities are important in understanding their individual lived experiences, and as such, we examine how sexism,

racism, classism, homophobia, transphobia, and ableism all inform Black girls' lives.

4. *Utilize community-based participatory research methods.* CBPR has been advocated as an approach for research to uproot inequities because it engages researchers, community members, and practitioners to work collaboratively to generate ideas and solutions. CBPR also builds collective power to implement those ideas and solutions. We integrate research, advocacy, and practice, using CBPR to help bridge the gaps that commonly exist between researchers and community members.

5. *Create opportunities for Black girls to thrive.* As we work to uproot the structural causes of the inequities that Black girls experience, we support and promote programs and approaches that create opportunities for Black girls to thrive in the face of these challenges. We emphasize empowerment models that promote self-efficacy and critical consciousness-raising. We recognize that Black girls engage in forms of resistance to oppression that are often minimized, silenced, or punished. We utilize a trauma-informed lens to understand how Black girls' experiences of personal and community trauma influence their reactions, behaviors, and perspectives. We celebrate the strengths of Black girls throughout everything we do.

Black Girls Advocacy and Leadership Alliance (BGALA)

Centering Black Girls: Theory and Values Guiding BGALA

As noted, integral to the Black Girls Equity Alliance is a commitment to centering the voices and experiences of Black girls and involving them in our collaborative advocacy efforts. However, this is easier said than done. We knew we could not simply invite girls to meetings with adults and expect them to be ready to contribute meaningfully when adults are not always accustomed to listening to young people and young people are not always accustomed to being heard. We had been considering ways to provide support and scaffolding for girls' participation in our efforts to change systems when we came across the Robert Wood Johnson Foundation's call for proposals for the second cohort of its Interdisciplinary Research Leaders (IRL) Program. The IRL Program supports teams of researchers and community partners in their collective development and capacity to engage in applied research to advance health equity. As noted in the introductory chapter to this book, the Robert Wood Johnson Foundation is focused on "building a culture of health," which means addressing the multiple, interconnected social determinants of health, as our advocacy and research attempt to do.

The themes for the 2017 IRL cohort were *resilience* and *youth violence prevention*. Given the extreme racial disproportionality in juvenile justice referrals of girls in our county and our articulated goal of having Black girls themselves as central actors in our systemic change efforts, we recognized the opportunity to propose an empowerment initiative for Black girls that would help prevent their justice system involvement by channeling their justified resistance to the oppression they face into collective action as partners in the BGEA. Thus, we designed a proposal that we titled, "Redefining Resilience and Reframing Resistance: Evaluation of a Violence Prevention and Health Promotion Empowerment Program for Black Girls," through which we could develop and evaluate a program to empower girls to participate in BGEA collective change initiatives.

We explicitly framed our work in a way that challenged individually-focused interpretations of the extreme racial disproportionality in juvenile justice referrals in our county, noting that many of Black girls' "delinquent" behaviors are attempts to protect themselves from harassment and abuse (which Black girls are more likely to experience than White girls, but from which they are less likely to be protected; Epstein, Blake, & González, 2017) and may also be expressions of frustration with adults who mistreat or dismiss them or who lack resources and opportunities. Though current narratives frequently define Black girls' resistance to oppression and injustice as delinquency, this resistance is an indicator of strength and resilience (Morris, 2016). Research has demonstrated that much of the differential treatment of Black girls in the justice system is a result of implicit and explicit biases and has documented that their criminalization, victimization, and marginalization have many detrimental impacts on their health.

We believed that one way to reduce these harms and inequities and to build a culture of health would be to involve Black girls in efforts to change the narratives about them. Unfortunately, many programs aimed at helping Black girls treat them as the problem, rather than acknowledging and addressing the fact that "problem behavior" is often a result of society's failure to protect them and of Black girls' own efforts to protect themselves, as well as their resistance to unjust treatment. Developed to challenge negative perceptions of Black girls, reduce their criminalization, and improve their health, the Black Girls Advocacy and Leadership Alliance (BGALA) was a collaboratively-developed program rooted in critical consciousness and Black feminism, designed to empower Black girls. While an important method and/or goal in much work with marginalized youth, "empowerment" has become a buzzword that is often vaguely defined and, at times, is operationalized in ways that focus solely on changing girls, despite the fact that empowerment theory demonstrates the necessity of simultaneously addressing the individual and institutional factors that contribute to social and health inequities (Bay-Cheng, 2012; Goodkind, 2009).

Thus, we designed the BGALA program to address both individual challenges and the societal failings that instigate them. By developing critical awareness of how societal inequities have contributed to the challenges they face and engaging in advocacy, girls would, we hypothesized, develop collective resilience. In contrast to an individually-focused conceptualization of resilience, which indicates thriving despite adversity and has the potential to put the responsibility for overcoming societal-level inequities on the shoulders of individual girls, collective resilience emphasizes the role of critical consciousness in enabling girls to identify the structural roots of what might first appear to be individual challenges and to work collectively to address these structural inequities (Goodkind, Brinkman, & Elliott, 2020).

We envisioned that this program and our associated research would have the potential to facilitate change in a number of important ways. First, it could help to reduce inequities in treatment and outcomes. Specifically, we planned to assess how advocacy training, restorative practices, and participatory research could reframe and channel girls' justified resistance to their unequal treatment toward meaningful social change. We also wanted to explore how the advocacy efforts in which the girls engaged could shift adults' narratives about Black girls and thus reduce their disparate treatment. In addition, we believed that our findings could advance theory about the mechanisms by which an empowerment approach could reduce inequities experienced by Black girls and provide empirical support for the effectiveness of participatory approaches that shift the focus from "'fixing' girls" to "engaging girls in 'fixing' society." By not only documenting the effectiveness of participatory approaches, but also delineating *how* they were effective, this project could provide research evidence for a model that could be useful in violence prevention and health promotion interventions with

Black girls and other marginalized youth. This evidence could then be used by service providers, justice system professionals, educators, and policymakers.

BGALA Program Design

We developed, piloted, and evaluated the Black Girls Advocacy and Leadership Alliance (BGALA) with high school girls in Pittsburgh, Pennsylvania, in 2018–2019. For the program, Gwen's Girls recruited high school girls both from within its existing participants and from schools and contacts throughout Pittsburgh and its other program sites. To be eligible, participants needed to be enrolled in high school; to be residents of Allegheny County, Pennsylvania; and to identify as Black girls. Girls were recruited by Gwen's Girls through their existing networks and beyond with a flyer that included the following questions:

> Have you ever wanted to speak up about something that was unfair but weren't sure how? Have you ever tried to speak up and you weren't listened to or got in trouble? Do you want to be part of a group of girls and young women working together to make things better? Would you like to develop ideas and skills to better understand and challenge injustice?

Girls were enrolled by Gwen's Girls staff and transportation was provided (via bus tickets or van) to sessions, which were held at local universities.

BGALA began in October 2018 and included weekly after-school sessions throughout the remainder of the 2018–2019 school year. Participants were provided with debit cards, to which $10 was added for each week they attended, in order to recognize the value of their time and effort and also to compensate for the fact that time spent at BGALA was time during which they could not be working. Each session began with dinner and was followed by 90 minutes of curriculum. The intent of each session was to focus on one or more aspects of the empowerment model, including positive gendered racial identity, critical reflection, political efficacy, and critical action. The curriculum included units focused on Black history, Black feminism, issues and inequities affecting Black girls, social justice, and research and advocacy skills. Approximately 30 girls participated in initial BGALA sessions. Because the girls came from throughout the county and many had school activities and family responsibilities, not all of those who began the program participated the entire year. In total, 15 girls aged 13–17 completed the year-long program.

Our interdisciplinary research team, which included the authors; graduate students in psychology, social work, and sociology; and Gwen's Girls staff, collected quantitative and qualitative data throughout the school year. Specifically, girls who joined the program completed detailed surveys prior to participating in BGALA, halfway through the school year, and at the end of the school year, and took part in individual in-depth interviews during the year, as well as a focus group at the end of the year. In addition, one of the graduate students took detailed field notes at the BGALA sessions throughout the year.

BGALA Evaluation Findings

Here we summarize a few of the key findings from our evaluation of the initial year of BGALA, which are described and discussed in more detail in a recent article in *Behavioral Medicine* (Goodkind, Brinkman, & Elliott, 2020). We began with the knowledge that Black girls in the U.S. experience high rates of discrimination and face numerous structural barriers. The participants in the BGALA program were no exception, with two-thirds attributing experiences of everyday discrimination to their race, over half to their gender, a third to their age, and a fourth to the income level. In addition, about 40% reported being unfairly discouraged from continuing their education by a teacher or advisor, and a similar percentage reported being unfairly stopped, searched, questioned, physically threatened, or abused by the police. In addition, two-thirds reported getting in trouble at school, including over 40% receiving a suspension and close to half experiencing disciplinary consequences for dress code violations.

Analyses of our survey data revealed no change in measures of individual resilience. Notably, scores on depression and delinquent behaviors stayed constant, which is a positive finding given that these generally increase with age during the teen years. We did find significant changes in measures related to the collective resilience promoted by the empowerment model. Specifically, there was an increase in perceptions of societal inequity and a decrease in adherence to neoliberal ideas that disregard systemic challenges, thus demonstrating the development of critical consciousness among participating girls. Analyses of our qualitative data showed that many participants critically reflected on their experiences of oppression, developed mutual support and positive gendered racial identity, and engaged in collective action. The development of critical consciousness is demonstrated in one participant's reflections:

> So [BGALA] impacted me ... because like now when somebody says something, I actually get it, like I actually understand it. And then when they say something, I say something back. ... Like when dudes say something about females that makes me so mad. Or when teachers say certain things about certain kids it just makes me mad.

Many participants described the development of a collective identity among Black girls. One said, "It's a fun way to learn about how you can make a change for not only yourself but for other women and girls just like you." An example of their collective action came at the end of the year, when a school that many of the participants attended created a more restrictive dress code and blamed the change on the broader efforts to create equity for Black girls, of which BGALA was a part. The girls were outraged and organized themselves to talk with the school administrators who ultimately made this change.

The evaluation demonstrated the effectiveness of our empowerment model in increasing critical reflection and positive gendered racial identity among Black girls, challenging traditional individualized models of resilience and reframing Black girls' resistance to injustice as an alternative, collective form of resilience. In the context of evidence of the harmful health effects of oppression and of behaviors defined as individually resilient among people experiencing such oppression, redefining resilience collectively and promoting it through empowerment interventions for Black girls and other marginalized youth are promising and important endeavors. Our next steps include using lessons learned from this evaluation (described subsequently) to enhance the BGALA program and to develop mechanisms for including girls in multiple years, perhaps with a component that enables returning girls to serve in mentoring/ facilitation roles that build on their previous experiences. In the remainder of this chapter, we share lessons learned about community-partnered research that we gleaned from a reflective conversation on our experiences of collaborative research for structural and systemic change.

Reflections

We decided to use the opportunity to contribute a chapter to this book to describe our process and to reflect on the past five years of collaborative research and advocacy. One of us developed a few questions to facilitate this process, and we met to collectively reflect on where we have been, where we are headed, what we have learned, and what might be useful to share with others engaging in similar types of collaborative endeavors. We begin by sharing a bit about each of us and what brought us to this work, and we then describe what emerged from our conversation that we believe might have relevance for other community–academic partnerships.

Who We Are

An integral part of community-engaged research is that it builds on the diverse strengths and experiences of all participants. Thus, who we are and where we have been are centered in our work. The Interdisciplinary Research Leaders program engaged us in a "River of Life" activity, where we mapped out the organizations, events, barriers, and facilitators involved in our collaborative work. Below, we include the "River of Life" map that we drew together (Figure 2.1), which illustrates the genesis of our collaborative work and of the BGALA program.

We share a commitment to equity work focused on eradicating gender- and race-based oppression—yet our personal and academic backgrounds are varied. We have complementary perspectives, knowledge, and experiences. Kathi, our community partner, has master's degrees in nursing and social work and a doctorate of nursing practice. She is a certified psychiatric nurse practitioner and community leader

Figure 2.1 River of Life map

and has supported our collaborative research with her extensive practice knowledge and experience, keeping it grounded in girls' experiences and facilitating connections with the community. Sara's expertise in social work, sociology, and women's studies brings an important focus on context and social justice. Britney contributes expertise in counseling psychology and women's studies, with an emphasis on youth activism.

Our collaboration is also enriched by our diverse backgrounds and experiences. Kathi is an African American woman who grew up in Pittsburgh, while Sara and Britney were raised in the western U.S. Britney is a White, multiracial woman whose Native American family traditions play an important part in her life, and Sara is a White woman who has lived internationally and contributes a global perspective. Our roles in this research built on our diverse perspectives and existing collaboration.

Kathi entered our partnership as the CEO of Gwen's Girls, an organization started by her mother, Gwendolyn J. Elliott, in 2002. Gwendolyn Elliott was the first African American woman to be a police commander in Pittsburgh and, upon her retirement from the police, she founded Gwen's Girls to support Black girls who she witnessed being marginalized throughout her career. Kathi stated: "Being an African American woman who grew up and continues to live in the same community as many of the girls in our program, I have first-hand experience of the systemic racial biases and barriers that they now encounter. I have also been impacted by the high rates of violence and trauma that have collectively become a public health epidemic. This has been my motivation to engage in this work."

Britney came to our collaboration as an associate professor of psychology engaged in social justice research with youths with a particular focus on eradicating identity-based harassment and discrimination in schools. She noted how existing school programming attempts to address "bullying" divorced from discussions of oppression, and stated: "Many schools employ the term 'bullying' to avoid addressing harassment and discrimination. Many then apply anti-bullying programs which claim to be 'value neutral' but in fact avoid the contexts related to social identities and power structures and utilize zero-tolerance policies, which can, in fact, punish victims of violence in schools." Thus, Britney is committed to centering race, gender, sexuality, and other aspects of social identity in her research, knowing that attempts to address violence without this explicit focus will not succeed.

Sara brought to the partnership an interdisciplinary background in social work and sociology. She wrote:

> I study and examine social service programs and systems that work with young people. I have a particular interest in young people's experiences in our educational, child welfare, and juvenile justice systems and how these systems both construct and meet the needs of the young people they serve. I became engaged with this work via an analysis of gender-specific services for girls in the juvenile justice system. While I did not begin this research with a specific focus on Black girls or girls of color, I have seen in the more than 15 years in which I have been doing this work that Black girls and other girls of color are overrepresented in many of these systems.

> Thus, I have conducted research to explore why this is the case, and we know, from the work of many researchers, that much of this is related to the structural racism and sexism that exist in our society. As a social work researcher, I am committed not only to documenting this oppression and inequity, but also to addressing it.

We are grateful for each other and for the opportunity to work collaboratively toward social justice. Beginning with an exploration of our individual backgrounds and experiences that led us to this work has enabled us to build relationships and trust and draw on the unique strengths and contributions of each of us. In the remainder of this chapter, we delineate and describe lessons learned through our collaboration that emerged in our reflective conversation.

Lessons Learned

1. *Relationships & trust are central.* This is not a new insight, but it is one that bears repeating and that emerged as a key component of our successful collaboration as we reflected together. We began our involvement in the Interdisciplinary Research Leaders (IRL) Program with an already strong relationship, and the intensive time together—as well as specific reflective activities structured into the program—facilitated by our participation in the IRL Program deepened our knowledge of each other's backgrounds and what brought us to this equity work, provided space for us to get to know each other's work styles, spend time together in less formal ways, and grow to enjoy and cherish our time together. As an added bonus, Kathi was able to recruit two additional Pittsburgh Steelers football fans by insisting that we find a fun place to watch the Steelers games that happened during our travels.

Through the conversations about our goals and commitments, we came to trust in our shared purpose. This strong foundation for our work together enabled us to weather the stress and conflicts that will inevitably surface in any sustained collaboration—particularly one in which the collaborators have many other demands on their time and attention.

2. *Be authentic.* The kind of equity work on which we partner tackles difficult issues, with a specific focus on racism. Often Britney and Sara would be asked why, as White women, we were engaged in this work focused on Black girls. Given our experiences in thinking and talking about this question, we agreed to facilitate a session with our IRL colleagues on being a White ally in racial justice work. While we all have different experiences, we believe that anti-oppression work is based on our shared humanity and the importance of human connections. There is a beautiful quote that expresses this idea from Lilla Watson, an indigenous Australian woman; she said, "If you have come here to help me, you are wasting your time, but if you have come because your liberation is bound up with mine, then let us work together." To make our multiracial coalition successful, we needed to be prepared for real and sometimes uncomfortable conversations that required us to be authentic with each other and with all of our partners. In particular, our engagement with the girls necessitated that we show up not as teachers, but as partners willing to challenge our own assumptions and beliefs in the same ways that we were asking girls to. It required that as adults, we listen more than talk, and for Britney and Sara, as White people, we listen even more and engage with cultural humility. Our honest reflection on each of our strengths and challenges allowed us to divide tasks in ways that built on

each of our unique strengths, at the same time that we created processes that enabled girls and adults alike to build new skills and push beyond our comfort zones. As we have worked together over time, our own and each other's strengths have become clearer, and we have developed a synergy and ease of communication that has enhanced our impact.

3. *Slow down.* A difficult lesson for our team has been that we need to slow down and take whatever time is needed both to build relationships and to engage in practices that allow for meaningful participation by girls and community partners. This is antithetical to the current, increasingly frenzied pace of academia and the pressure that researchers experience to publish as much and as quickly as possible, which makes slowing down structurally difficult. By extension, it is also antithetical to the White capitalist patriarchal mindset that governs so much of what happens in the U.S., including academia. At times, the distressing extent of the systemic inequities we are working to address has led us to rush—rush to begin the BGALA program, rush to complete analyses for dissemination, rush to show up in spaces we are not yet ready to appear. Our hurry is motivated by the urgency of the problems we seek to address. Yet, the intractable nature of these inequities has led us to recognize and honor that we are in this for the long haul and we must, therefore, pace ourselves. At some crucial points in this work, we felt tension between the timeline we had laid out ahead of time and what would actually be best for the BGALA program participants; at times, we erred on the side of beginning activities for which we were not yet ready. Decisions about timeline, what to prioritize, and so on must be made continually and collaboratively, as unexpected challenges present themselves, even if it means missing

certain opportunities. We have had to (begrudgingly) accept that we cannot do it all and that the change we seek will not happen overnight, and, in learning these lessons, we have become more able to adapt to unforeseen changes and challenges along the way.

4. *Be flexible.* Along with taking the time to engage with purpose and intention, we have learned that we must be ready to adapt to unanticipated opportunities and challenges. This can be challenging in academic and funding environments that require detailed plans, but it is a necessary component of CBPR that centers on community collaboration. It is also an uncomfortable approach for some of us, given that traditional academic education and the structure of many institutions promotes and rewards careful planning and adherence to plans. We have learned through our work together that we will make mistakes, have disagreements, and face unforeseen challenges. To withstand these challenges, we need flexibility that allows us to let go of smaller things, learn new approaches, and creatively adapt. As Britney noted in our reflective conversation, such flexibility "creates moments of opportunity for things to emerge." Britney has helped us to incorporate the flexible approach introduced by adrienne maree brown in *Emergent Strategy: Shaping Change, Changing Worlds* (2017) to enhance our collaborative work.

5. *Engage in work that is community driven rather than researcher driven.* Our work is grounded in the community—not in the sense of one specific neighborhood but in place-based specifics that drive systemic inequities shaping Black girls' experiences in our locality. Community-partnered research and advocacy recognizes, as Britney stated in our conversation, that "you can't just show up and talk to people for an hour and understand" the community-specific phenomena you are committed to addressing. History and social

context shape specific manifestations of societal inequities, and local knowledge and experience are central to addressing them. Our collaborative work has always been driven by community goals and needs and not by researchers' interests. This has been relatively easy to center in our partnership because our collaboration emerged through invitations directed to Britney and Sara to join the advisory board of the Gwendolyn J. Elliott Institute at Gwen's Girls. Often, researchers begin with research questions and seek community agencies and organizations where they can answer these questions. However, we believe that ideally, the questions and goals emerge from the community and that the partnership is negotiated in ways that recognize and honor the differences in academic and community perspectives. This is not to say that we should ignore the interests and requirements of academia; indeed, the partnership must be mutually beneficial so that academic partners can meet the expectations placed on them at the same time that we work to make academia more supportive of CBPR and thus, more relevant to the community and broader world.

We write this chapter at a moment of intense hope and fear. We are in the midst of a pandemic that has hit marginalized communities particularly hard and has forced all of us to rethink and reorganize how we do almost everything. We are also in a moment when continued structural violence against Black people in the U.S. has led to renewed resistance and a commitment by many to endeavor to make all of our institutions antiracist. At the same time, Donald Trump, the former occupant of the White House, issued a directive while he was still in power that forbid the use of federal funding to train government employees with teachings about White privilege or using critical race theory. He also threatened to end federal funding to schools that engage in such teachings. Though current president Joe Biden has rescinded this directive, the influence of Trump's reactionary rhetoric persists. Clearly, we need our connections and collaborations more than ever, because we will not weather these challenges and make the needed societal changes alone. We cannot think of a time when our collective resilience was as necessary as it is now.

In our local work, we have begun to shift the narrative and to garner attention for our collaborative research and advocacy to the point that now, many people are seeking us out to join our efforts. We were ready to contribute to the renewed national call to address racist police violence in response to the horrific murders of George Floyd and Breonna Taylor and the resulting national push for police-free schools because we have been collectively engaged in this work. Our newest BGEA report, *Understanding and Addressing Institutionalized Inequity: Disrupting Pathways to Juvenile Justice for Black Youth in Allegheny County*, highlights the role of school police in funneling Black youths into the juvenile justice system and offers concrete suggestions for change, which will move us toward the elimination of the racial disproportionality in juvenile justice referrals that motivated the development of the BGALA program. Because of BGALA, girls were eager and ready to participate in advocacy for police-free schools and in the webinars that Gwen's Girls has been holding over Zoom during the pandemic to highlight the experiences of Black girls during this time and to catalyze local action to ensure our systems are adequately supporting them. We have a constant refrain in our work: stop trying to fix the *girls*, and instead focus on fixing the *systems*. When we make space for the joy and power that Black girls can bring to these systemic change efforts, we shift the narrative, enabling policymakers and system actors to see Black girls as valuable, essential members of the community. Further, by centering Black girls in this work, we also enhance the effectiveness of our collaborative work to build a culture of health and make the community better for all.

References

Allegheny County Health Department, UPMC Children's Hospital of Pittsburgh, & University of Pittsburgh School of Public Health. (2014). *Healthy Allegheny teen survey*. https://www.alleghenycounty.us/Health-Department/Resources/Data-and-Reporting/Chronic-Disease-Epidemiology/Healthy-Allegheny-Teen-Survey.aspx

Allegheny County JPO. (2020). *Data analysis from Melanie King of referrals to the Juvenile Probation Office*. Allegheny County Juvenile Probation Office.

Bay-Cheng, L. Y. (2012). Recovering empowerment: De-personalizing and re-politicizing adolescent female sexuality. *Sex Roles, 66*, 713–717.

Brinkman, B. G., Goodkind, S., Elliott, K., Joseph, A., & Doswell, W. M. (2019). *Advocating for equity for Black girls: The formation of the Black Girls Equity Alliance*. Black Girls Equity Alliance.

brown, a. m. (2017). *Emergent strategy: Shaping change, changing worlds*. AK Press.

Crenshaw, K., Ocen, P., & Nanda, J. (2015). *Black girls matter: Pushed out, overpoliced and underprotected*. African American Policy Forum.

Elliott, K., Goodkind, S., Makoshi, G., & Shook, J. (2020). *Understanding and addressing institutionalized inequity: Disrupting pathways to juvenile justice for Black youth in Allegheny County*. Black Girls Equity Alliance.

Epstein, R., Blake, J., & González, T. (2017). *Girlhood interrupted: The erasure of Black girls' childhood*. Georgetown University Law Center on Poverty and Inequality.

Goodkind, S. (2009). "You can be anything you want, but you have to believe it": Commercialized feminism in gender-specific programs for girls. *Signs, 34*, 387–422.

Goodkind, S. (2016). *Inequities affecting Black girls in Pittsburgh and Allegheny County*. The Heinz Endowments and the Pittsburgh Foundation.

Goodkind, S., Brinkman, B. G., & Elliott, K. (2020). Redefining resilience and reframing resistance: Empowerment programming with Black girls to address societal inequities. *Behavioral Medicine, 46*, 317–329.

Morris, M. W. (2016). *Pushout: The criminalization of Black girls in schools*. The New Press.

Puzzanchera, C., Sladky, A., & Kang, W. (2021). "Easy Access to Juvenile Populations: 1990–2020." Online. Available: https://www.ojjdp.gov/ojstatbb/ezapop/

Sickmund, M., Sladky, A., & Kang, W. (2021). "Easy Access to Juvenile Court Statistics: 1985–2019" Online. Available: https://www.ojjdp.gov/ojstatbb/ezajcs/

Chapter 3

Insights from Project Youth MIND

Building a Virtual Youth Community during a Health and Racial Pandemic

Michelle C. Chatman and Ryan T. Wright

This work was conducted as part of the Interdisciplinary Research Leaders program and comprises the reflections and insights gained from implementing a community-engaged, youth violence intervention in Washington, D.C. The nascent program, Project Youth MIND (which stands for Mindfulness Integration for Nonviolent Development), is introduced as a framework for supporting the social-emotional development of Black youths through a mindfulness-based curriculum that reflects their cultural identities and cultivates a deeper awareness of social justice. The chapter chronicles the implementation of the intervention from 2019–2020 amid the COVID-19 pandemic and social unrest in response to racialized violence. The authors provide their unique vantage points on the importance of embodying tenets of mindfulness, as a cultural anthropologist and a budding male counselor, when sharing such approaches with youths. Lessons learned and promising youth feedback are presented to reinforce the need for more in-person and virtual healing spaces for youths in urban settings.

Introduction

This chapter is about our journey with Project Youth MIND (Mindfulness Integration for Nonviolent Development), the youth violence prevention program we piloted in Washington, D.C., under the aegis of the Interdisciplinary Research Leaders (IRL) program, one of the signature leadership programs of the Robert Wood Johnson Foundation (RWJF) designed to advance health equity in communities across America. The IRL Program recruits cohorts of three-member research teams comprised of a community partner and two academics who work together over a three-year period developing their research leadership skills while simultaneously implementing community-engaged research projects. Michelle C. Chatman, Associate Professor of Criminal Justice at the University of the District of Columbia (UDC); Sharon T. Alston, Assistant Professor of Social Work at Norfolk State University (NSU), and K. Ivy Hylton, Founder and Director of Youth and Families in Crisis, LLC, and the MA'AT Training Institute for Restorative Justice, were members of the IRL Program (Cohort 2) from 2017 to 2020. Ryan Wright, graduate student in the Master of Arts in Rehabilitative Counseling program at UDC, served as the primary graduate assistant to the project.

Project Youth MIND (PYM) is designed to prevent youth engagement in violence and promote health and resilience through an integrated model of mindfulness, restorative justice practices, the arts, and social justice education, particularly for Black youths. The PYM intervention employs an ecological model in helping youths examine the multiple spheres of influence that shape their ideas and behaviors as it relates to managing peer and family relationships, handling conflict and difficult emotions, navigating adolescence, and dealing with the challenges of daily life. PYM was designed as a year-long, in-person, after-school intervention for youths between the ages of 14 and 15. Yet, as discussed in the unfolding narrative, the project underwent multiple adaptations, as is common for community-engaged endeavors, and was eventually piloted as a virtual program during the tumultuous summer of 2020 in the midst of the COVID-19 pandemic and protests for justice across the U.S. and around the world.

PYM is informed by the varied disciplines of anthropology, criminal justice, and social work, in its effort to address the social determinants of health and safety for Black youths. Components of the PYM model (restorative justice, mindfulness, creative arts, and social justice education) have been shown to support positive youth development when offered as stand-alone interventions; yet, our project asked how an integration of these elements, offered in a culturally responsive context, might support the healthy development of Black youths. School-based restorative justice programs offer students a mechanism for building community and settling conflicts. They have become a popular approach for addressing school-based disciplinary issues and have been used as an alternative to youth suspensions and expulsions, to which Black youths are disproportionately subjected (Center for Educational Statistics, 2015). For example, when conflict arises between students or when a student exhibits disruptive behavior in class, the situation is resolved, to the extent possible, through a restorative process such as a peace circle, family group conference, or mediation. Some schools also host mindfulness or restorative rooms where students can receive support with processing their feelings; they are also often allowed time to cool down before returning to class. The aim of this approach is to provide a restorative response to situations rather than relying on exclusionary practices, which lead to academic loss, and place youths at greater risk of violence and justice system involvement. Such approaches are also being used to transform school climates and cultures from punitive environments to those that are trauma-informed and holistic in their support of students facing challenges.

A growing body of research demonstrates the benefits of mindfulness in reducing stress, anxiety, and depression while simultaneously promoting concentration, awareness, focus, and empathy in youth and emerging adults. Here, mindfulness is conceptualized as the practice of maintaining a nonjudgmental, present-moment awareness of one's internal state (thoughts and emotions) as well as the external environment of sounds, sights, and other stimuli (Mendelson, 2010; Semple, 2017). School-based mindfulness programs have proliferated in the last decade and research shows promise that these programs provide youths with skills to self-regulate, thereby making them more available for learning and positive peer engagement while simultaneously supporting their overall well-being. These outcomes have been achieved primarily through secular mindfulness meditation practices and yoga. Yet, we believe this work requires a lens that is both culturally responsive and focuses on social justice, as we know that structural inequities are the cause of the suffering of many of our young people. Empowering youths with mindfulness and social-emotional competencies, while commendable, is limited in changing policies and practices that disadvantage Black and other youths of color, and poor youths. The mindfulness movement may also benefit from giving more consideration to the culturally specific ways that Black youths and families have sustained their resilience and centeredness throughout history and in the face of contemporary social challenges (Utsey, 2000). We see PYM as offering a glimpse into that body of wisdom, giving us an opportunity to center our efforts for Black youth and family well-being on the cultural ethos of the Black diaspora.

Hip hop, spoken word, poetry, and art are potent forms of creative expression and empowering pedagogies for engaging Black youths, allowing them to convey personal and social-political messages around identity, oppression, freedom, justice, and power (Keith, 2019; Love, 2016). We integrated these elements into PYM with the hopes that it would offer youths a different way of relating to themselves and their peers with the combined values of restorative justice, culturally-responsive mindfulness and contemplative skills, social justice education, and opportunities for pro-social engagement; youths will internalize coping skills to resolve conflicts and manage anxiety and stress in healthy, nonviolent ways. Further, we hope that this intervention will provide youths with a critical lens through which they can view the various systems that touch their lives and the lives of their families, as well as their communities, such as the education, social services, and justice systems.

Race, Resilience, and Black Youths

Resilience is commonly thought of as one's ability to bounce back from challenging situations or to persevere through adversity. In the social and behavioral sciences, we discuss resilience as a characteristic or state that can be attained when protective factors exceed risk factors, thereby advancing opportunities for thriving. Yet, Black youths are affected by manifold forms of structural racism, which has been strongly correlated with adversity (Chatman, 2019; Love, 2016; Morris, 2016). Structural racism directly impacts Black youths' ability to thrive as many live in communities impacted by violence, crime, unemployment, underfunded schools, and concentrated poverty, which places them at risk for negative outcomes. Black families and youths continue to experience significant racial disparities in most social indicators of well-being. Black youth violence, and the loss of Black youth potential, exist as parts of a larger ecosystem of violence and historical oppression against which Black families continue to struggle. This fact is rooted in a history of bondage that lasted for centuries; race-based brutality; and federal, state, and local government policies that have maintained a system of White supremacy that devalues Black lives. Considering this reality, how, then, do we define and support resilience for Black youths?

We argue that a historically grounded analysis of resilience is needed when considering the condition of Black youths in the United States. This analysis must acknowledge the legacy of racism and oppression in shaping life-outcomes for Black youth. We conceptualize resilience as the ability to access one's personal, family, and community resources to support thriving. Rooted in community and culture, we see resilience as actionable, as praxis. We see Project Youth MIND as a resource for helping youths cultivate greater internal capacities while also developing external protective factors, connected to place and community, to support their health and safety. We realize that creating conditions of thriving for Black youths requires a multi-pronged approach. As we collectively mobilize against unjust racist structures, policies, and practices, so too must we support youths with immediate tools and resources to help them navigate an unjust world.

Authors and Intentions

Having worked closely together over 2 and a half years on the PYM intervention, we offer this chapter as Black scholars, educators, public servants, contemplative practitioners, and caregivers of Black children, who are committed to healing and justice for the families and youths in our hometown of Washington, D.C. We seek to accomplish several aims with this offering. We share here how our personal journeys with mindfulness and other contemplative approaches support our individual resilience, and how we integrate these practices into our work with Black youths. We discuss some of the challenges we encountered on this project and how the embodiment of compassion and resilience served as resources for our grounding and inquiry. We briefly outline the process for adapting Project Youth MIND for virtual delivery to D.C.'s youths during a time of immense chaos, uncertainty, and fear resulting from COVID-19 and racialized violence in America, as evidenced by the murders of George Floyd, Breonna Taylor, Ahmaud Arbery, and other innocent, unarmed Black people.

Another goal of this chapter is to give voice to the spiritual or contemplative dimension of our researcher identity. We deem it crucial to expose this aspect of ourselves given that our research centers on the social and emotional wellbeing of youths. In our view, it is essential that researchers aspiring to do this kind of work with youths be deeply in touch with their own interior. Thus, we lay bare our positionalities and intersectional identities, as we believe they strengthen the credibility and authenticity of our work. We contend that a mature sense of personal and social awareness is a requirement for doing social emotional learning (SEL) and mindfulness work with youths, particularly with Black youths, who have been historically marginalized and continue to be devalued in our society. Further, we discuss how our contemplative lives have deepened by virtue of our experience with the project, inviting us into closer communion with our contemplative lives. We write this chapter after having just completed the Youth MIND pilot, which consisted of six weeks of virtual engagement with 44 youths across D.C. Thus, this essay is largely a reflective account of our experiences and major lessons learned which, we hope, will be instructive for individuals doing similar work.

Michelle C. Chatman—Authenticity and Mindfulness

Our lives constitute layers of histories, experiences, and influences that shape us. As such, an authentic life demands that we conduct a self-excavation to know who we truly are (McLaurin, 2001; Sealey-Ruiz, 2017). I have multiple identities. I am a cisgender, Black feminist anthropologist, decolonizing contemplative scholar-activist, Orisha priest, artist, entrepreneur, matriarch, and daughter of the African Diaspora. I was born and raised in all-Black neighborhoods in Washington, D.C. The places where I grew up were under-resourced by government investment, but financed by Black love and grit. My parents worked hard to advance our family from a subsidized apartment to a rented house to eventual homeownership. This research takes place in my hometown of Washington, D.C., a city that once enjoyed a reputation as a mecca for Black culture, arts, politics, and upward mobility. Like many other urban enclaves, D.C. lived through the crack epidemic that ravaged Black neighborhoods and claimed hundreds of Black lives in the '80s and '90s. I grew up during that era and like many others, have lost friends, relatives, and students to senseless violence—including my 17-year-old brother, Abdullah R. Coghill. School, books, the arts, and a loving family who set high expectations for me sustained my imagination and resilience as a D.C. youth. After graduating from college, I traveled to The Gambia, West Africa, annually for five consecutive summers to teach and work with vocational school youths. I regard this experience as the genesis of my contemplative journey and seminal in my process of African cultural reclamation.

My inner life is enriched by mindfulness meditation, African spirituality, prayer, music, time in nature, and writing. These approaches have helped me overcome numerous challenges and have facilitated my self-awareness, career choice, and social activism. I regularly include mindfulness and other contemplative approaches in my teaching and public presentations. Yet, my ultimate goal in this arena is not merely to enable Black people to withstand the violence of racism and oppression through mindfulness. Rather, it is to facilitate personal health, safety, and greater self-mastery as we work collectively to dismantle systems of harm and create structures of healing in our communities and society. I have nurtured an interest in the intersection of contemplative practices (including mindfulness), culture, and social justice for several years. As I promote mindful awareness among Black youths, I choose to remind them of their inherent value and power as a counternarrative to the dominant frames portrayed in the media. I share with them stories of my upbringing in D.C., some of the triumphs and challenges of my life, and the family members and students I have lost to violence. I teach them about the internalization of White supremacy and how it has perpetuated multigenerational traumas in Black families, which, along with institutional racism, attempts to thwart our full humanity and liberation (Magee, 2019; Menakem, 2017). And I disclose how the exploration of my own family trauma and deep, continuous engagement in my personal healing have opened vistas to joyful growth in my career and family life. I have found that this kind of "showing up" is absolutely necessary for building authentic connections with youth, as many of them have been impacted by very similar realities. My work with youths is bi-directional. I benefit tremendously from their openness, curiosity, and sometimes skepticism about mindful approaches, and in turn they make me a better teacher, mother, and servant-leader. My greatest hope is that by journeying together, even for the few weeks of the PYM program, we can all open ourselves to a deeper well of wisdom, healing, and imagination for our lives and communities than we ever thought possible.

Ryan T. Wright—My Passport to Mindfulness

Growing up in Washington, D.C., I often heard people speak of D.C. males as being flashy, aggressive, narrow-minded, and living a "thug life." Although these stereotypes were never associated with me, they impacted how I perceived and projected my sense of self. As a youth I was reticent about sharing my interests in electronic music and Korean food, or my curiosity about Buddhism out of fear of ridicule and rejection. At one point in my life, I had grown discontented and began to feel removed from my environment and social circle. I also became emotionally drained from managing the discrepancy between how I saw myself and how I experienced myself. Traveling proved a remedy for managing this chasm, allowing me to view myself through a different cultural lens and build relationships with others where I felt validated and understood. In the last decade, I've had the opportunity to travel to a dozen countries. My experiences living in South Korea and Lebanon have been instrumental in helping me cultivate my mindfulness practice and shaping how I conceptualize myself as a Black man. This increased awareness of how I relate to others transferred into an awareness of my relationship with myself.

Living in South Korea showed me how to put into practice the value of "other-esteem," which denotes an awareness of the feelings, beliefs, and attitudes of others (Corey, Corey, & Muatori, 2018). The scale on which I experienced other-esteem while in South Korea allowed me to explicitly observe the nuances in behavior that communicated care for others, such as pouring another's drink for them. My travels to Beirut, Lebanon, had an indelible impression upon reshaping my awareness of masculinity—particularly, my level of comfort with men entering my personal space. As a youth, I had internalized rigid gender norms that deemed physical contact between men (beyond a greeting or display of physical dominance) as being feminine or weak. Yet, in Beirut, I noticed that men interacted with each other in close personal distance and would often put their arms around each other when talking, or even give an impromptu shoulder massage. I recall having very mixed feelings when offered one of these impromptu massages. It was later explained to me that this was a cultural signal of expressing care, concern, and friendship. This discrete encounter showed me the flexible nature of masculinity and how proxemics vary from culture to culture. Thus began my internal process of more deeply examining the lens through which I viewed and analyzed "masculine" behaviors.

In my work as a counselor, I aim to build a connection with youths through understanding their subjective worldviews and values, and by emulating a contemplative attitude. My therapeutic approach with Black males includes supporting their multidimensional nature. I aspire to help Black men and youths understand that we are irreducible (Hannon & Vereen, 2016), and comprise many identities that encapsulate the depth of our talents, interests, and experiences.

My professional identity as a Black counselor has been shaped by the existential-humanistic values of self-actualization, introspection, and meaning (Yalom, 1980); these are values that I consider an extension of myself, and are integral to the process of helping others create a meaningful existence. In my work with Black youths, I often communicate these values in a calm and nondirective manner. This approach has been met with resistance from former colleagues with whom I've worked, who assert that a loud, stern, and somewhat aggressive demeanor is more effective with Black male youths. Yet, this approach is counter to the aim of building a therapeutic rapport. Through my professional work, I aim to offer Black male youths the space that I was not afforded as a young Black male—the freedom to refute rigid, racialized gender norms around Black masculinity and the space to express as a multidimensional, complex human being.

Designing Youth MIND—Chatman's Reflection

The three-year experience of designing and implementing this project can be characterized by two words: "pivots" and "adaptations." A number of dynamics required our team to go back to the proverbial drawing board on more than one occasion. Initially, I designed PYM as a year-long, school-based intervention for incoming 9th graders who would be starting high school. Dr. Graham,[1] the principal of the school where we had hoped to pilot PYM, was a fierce advocate for restorative justice and had a solid, long-standing relationship with our IRL community research partner, Dr. K. Ivy Hylton. During our pre-application planning stage, Dr. Hylton and I met with Dr. Graham, who was energetic, deeply committed to the students and families she served, and enthusiastic about PYM's potential to positively impact her students. We applied to the IRL program with the intention of offering the intervention at her school. After being accepted into IRL, we spent September 2017–December 2017 refining our research plan and becoming acclimated to the IRL fellowship program. Between January 2018 and June 2018, we worked to cultivate a relationship with Dr. Graham and the school staff through emails, video conferences, and school visits.

---

1. A pseudonym has been substituted for this person's real name.

With the assistant principal, we had begun strategizing ways to earn parent and student buy-in and broader community engagement. Yet, our momentum was curtailed when there were sudden staffing changes at the school and Dr. Graham was reassigned. This was an incredible disruption to our plans and to the school community. When new school leadership was appointed, they opted to focus on building internal school capacity and subsequently, our partnership was suspended. Our efforts to identify another school partner over the next months were to no avail. Penetrating a school proved to be more difficult than I had anticipated and revealed some of the challenges with doing community-engaged research with other complex systems that have their own sets of priorities, personnel, expectations, pressures, and motives.

The challenges we faced with finding a host site were also compounded by a protracted Institutional Review Board (IRB) process and at times, some very challenging team dynamics. Unlike some of the other IRL teams in our cohort, we were relatively new to each other and had never worked together as a trio. It took time and effort to get on the same page and find our stride—an experience in research team resilience! Further, since my institution managed the grant for the team, I was handling our administrative responsibilities; this task was quite demanding and at times, a source of consternation. The stage and health of a team's relationship shape how they perceive and manage setbacks and turning points on a given project. This became strikingly clear during the IRL experience. While the PYM pilot was in somewhat of a holding pattern, we prioritized the team relationship and sought a team coach while simultaneously searching for prospective youth groups with whom we could partner.

An opportune pivot emerged in May 2019, when IRL Fellow Dr. Sharon T. Alston reached out to her contact in the Teen Programs

Office in the D.C. Department of Parks and Recreation (DCDPR). Dr. Alston had a long-standing relationship with the agency and had lent them her youth development expertise on several occasions. After multiple conversations with staff from the Teen Programs, they invited us to share some of the Youth MIND modules with a subset of their youth population through their I.M.A.G.E. Camp summer program. Although PYM was designed as an after-school intervention, this interesting pivot was an opportunity not to be missed. We realized the immense value of trying out some of the PYM modules by offering them as workshops with the I.M.A.G.E. camp teens, which would allow us to get real-time youth feedback on the program content and delivery method. Thus, we accepted the invitation and excitedly began planning for our PYM summer community engagement.

Testing the Waters—Project Youth MIND 2019

With our welcome from the DCDPR, we offered a set of theme-based, in-person workshops from the PYM curriculum to assess the feasibility of the program model. The following paragraphs provide a summary of our activities and lessons learned. We conducted Youth MIND at two DCDPR sites in the area of D.C. called Ward 7, which has a predominantly Black, low-income, working-class population. We delivered sessions on mindfulness, adolescent brain development, trauma and stress, restorative circles, yoga, and spoken word. Each session was offered in workshop format with an experiential component such as role playing, team challenges, and interactive exercises. We conducted seven PYM sessions at each site between July 2 and July 25, 2019. Sessions were held on Tuesday and Thursday with the exception of the July 4th federal holiday. We offered 14 hours of programming at each site, totaling 28 hours of total programming to 35 students between the ages of 14 and 16. Each session lasted two hours and the content was identical at each site. At 83%, the majority of the participants were Black males. Black females comprised 17% of the program participants. Youths in these camps were also participants in D.C.'s summer youth employment program, and PYM was part of their work assignment at the recreation center.

We began each session with an opening circle and made a custom of shaking hands and making eye contact with the youths in the morning and afternoon sessions as a way of giving each of them a bit of individualized attention. We'd chat a bit, compliment what they were wearing or their disposition, or mention some other light topic to help make connection. They mostly returned our smiles and small talk. We then would go into an energizer or game such as Zip, Zap, Zoom; Youth MIND trivia (based on program content or staff facts); or Buzz (a numbers game). After a tone of fun and openness had been achieved, we would share the agenda for the day. We did this to create an atmosphere of ease and connection between the students and the PYM team members, who were outsiders.

We frequently sat in a circle or U-shaped formation in the program to reinforce the principles of restorative justice. The circle conveys equanimity, mutual respect, and connection, which are values we wanted to amplify. Over the duration of the program, youths engaged with a multigenerational team of ten African American adults (regular staff and consultants) who ranged in profession, age, gender expression, and life experience. Of those adults, there were four men and six women. Among their expertise were a retired fire department commander; a mindfulness and yoga teacher; a Black male school counselor; and two female undergraduate psychology students.

The students had a range of experiences over our weeks together. They had spoken word class once weekly and yoga twice weekly. We taught a mindfulness practice each week and by the end of the session, students had learned a basic belly breathing technique; a body scan, which is an exercise of moving one's awareness to different areas of the body from head to toe; a three-minute mindfulness meditation using a sand timer; and several yoga poses. UDC undergraduate students Sparkle Perry and Labrina Long led a session on colors and mood, sharing a bit about the Vedic teaching of the chakra energy systems. Students were asked to paint pictures reflecting their moods, hopes, and dreams on small 4 x 6 canvases, and were provided with materials to do so. Afterward, they discussed what their works of art were intended to convey. In the restorative justice workshop, students created flash skits, chants, and commercials based on a brief lesson about restorative justice, which yielded lots of laughter and creativity. Youths learned the purpose of the talking piece in the restorative circle and practiced using it. They also experienced a sound healing session with crystal bowls led by our community partner and IRL Fellow, Dr. K. Ivy Hylton.

Some of the students resisted the programming being offered. Several were preoccupied with their cellphones, which we had to continuously remind them to put away. Yet, the majority of students seemed receptive to the sessions and also seemed to have embraced us as caring, or at least tolerable, adults who wanted to offer something constructive. Engagement for many students strengthened over time. For example, in the second week, a few youths were beginning to lead brief mindfulness practices and demonstrate yoga poses with the guidance of the instructor. After each of our sessions, we debriefed and served snacks; this was also a valuable time to build trust and community to further strengthen engagement.

Social justice was seamlessly embedded in the spoken word sessions where master poet Joseph Green led students in writing exercises around identity, racism, and community violence. The prompts led students to share personal experiences like that of Lonnell,[2] an aspiring boxer, who spoke of the many times he'd been racially profiled by police officers. He recounted being stopped and questioned many times as he walked around the city. The smooth-skinned 14-year-old with gold-tipped dreadlocks shared that he was glad he had learned to just be calm and "stay cool," understanding that not doing so could possibly jeopardize his future.

To obtain students' feedback on the modules, we asked them to write anonymous comments on small index cards after each session. This was a nonthreatening way to obtain their input. At the end of the program, we administered a two-page, 15-item, anonymous survey where youths assessed the various components of the program. We also held a two-hour debrief session with approximately 20 students who were invited back to share their deeper insights and suggestions for the program based on the completed evaluation forms. The recreation center site managers and PYM team selected the youths for the debriefing session based on their engagement and cooperation during the actual program. In short, their suggestions were: 1) Keep Project Youth MIND as a summer program instead of an after-school intervention, which would interfere with sports and after-school jobs; 2) Include more project-based and hands-on learning opportunities; 3) Keep the program fun and interactive; and 4) Retain the sessions on the teen brain, understanding feelings, and managing emotions and stress. Several students shared that although they learned a bit about the body and brain in health class, they would

---

2. A pseudonym has been substituted for this person's real name.

benefit from more in-depth teaching on the subject and a greater understanding about how stress affects youths physically and emotionally.

Black Males and Mindfulness—Wright's Reflection on 2019

Working with Project Youth MIND presented me with an opportunity to expand my awareness of mindfulness and my cultural identity. As I began to reflect on my personal journey as a Black male and therapist, I wondered how the youths would receive me. Honestly, I harbored some trepidation about being accepted by the teen boys and worried about whether or not I would be able to relate to them in a meaningful way. I questioned which aspects of my identity I could bring to the forefront in my work—whether I should stay surface-level and engage around the arenas of sports and popular culture, or if I should attempt to connect on a deeper emotional level. I asked if those were mutually exclusive domains. I became acutely aware of how our actions either facilitated or became a hindrance to providing youths with a reflective, contemplative experience.

Teaching mindfulness-based practices to youths in D.C. presented me with both challenges and opportunities. One challenge that we had to contend with was offering the intervention during the summer. The didactic instruction reminded youths of school and they sometimes rebelled and became disengaged during the lesson. Once, while teaching a lesson on the Triune brain model and trauma, I noticed that females were engaged, but a few males actively talked and disrupted the lesson. I invited some of the males to assist me with drawing the brain models on the whiteboard, but they continued to talk loudly and resist participating in the lesson. Furthermore, males were more likely to participate and take initiative in active mindfulness lessons such as yoga or mindful movement; females, on the other hand, were engaged in reflective and contemplative practices such as meditation and deep breathing. This observation was supported by previous research suggesting that females outperform males on tasks related to observing, while males do better on skills related to acting with awareness (Alispahic & Hasanbegovic-Anic, 2017).

Chatman constantly reminded staff not to verbally force or coerce students into being active participants in the program, but rather, to allow them to experience the intervention at their own individual paces. She cautioned us to be aware of how we communicated with the youths, especially when we were frustrated by the cavalier level of engagement they would sometimes display. Redirecting a student with a polite request rather than a stern demand went against conventional wisdom regarding working with teens. Most staff members with prior experience working with youth from D.C. attested to the need to be stern so that we would not "get run over" by their assertive behavior. Yet, our program chose not to privilege adultism, but rather, to trust that we could invite youths to make choices to support their corrective actions that were grounded in mutual respect and maturity.

Another challenge that worked against the male students' capacity to fully experience the activities in the Summer 2019 program were rigid gender norms that dictated "appropriate behavior" (Marasco, 2005). As a warm-up, students were asked to participate in a mindful eating activity. The activity was presented as a way to become more aware of how people experience their food, which could lead to healthier and more satisfying food choices. As the activity progressed, students were verbally guided on how to eat a mint, while attending to the physical properties of the object. When students were guided to move the mint around on their tongue and refrain from chewing and swallowing it, the males sexualized the activity and remarked that it was "gay." This created a barrier (Kupers, 2018) that prevented males from fully experiencing the benefits of mindfulness activities.

These experiences caused me to become acutely aware of the need to fully embody mindfulness values as we attempt to teach them to students. Displaying incongruence between what a person says and does will quickly lead to losing credibility in the eyes of young people. As a contemplative practice, mindfulness should be a way of being that entails awareness, focus, and attunement to one's self and others. Acting in ways that communicate hostility and contempt can harm and undermine trusting connections between youths and adults. Adults must be aware of their word choices, volume, and most importantly, their intention when communicating with youths from a mindful perspective. Even when addressing oppositional teens, we strove to communicate with compassion and directness. In reflecting on the first year of PYM, I learned that teaching mindfulness to urban D.C. teens is a process that entails situating the practice of mindfulness within the proper social-cultural context. For us, this meant utilizing familiar mediums such as hip-hop, trap music, social media, spoken word, and art to teach more novel concepts such as body scanning, crystal bowl meditation, and mindful eating. These mediums gave students the platforms and spaces to explore their emotions and communicate their personal narratives of being Black teens from D.C. I found this to be the most impactful aspect of the program in our first year.

2020 Project Youth MIND Pilot

The 2019 Project Youth MIND experience gave us some incredibly useful information that we integrated into our planning for the actual pilot intervention. With the insights from the summer 2019 community engagement with DCDPR, we made slight modifications to our IRB application and secured approval in December 2019. In early 2020, we formalized our partnership with DCDPR and were ramping up to begin planning logistics for a summer 2020 pilot when COVID-19 halted our plan. District of Columbia government agencies, including city-run neighborhood recreation centers, closed in March 2020. Soon, Mayor Muriel Bowser issued strict stay-at-home orders to help curtail the spread of the virus. When we learned that schools, recreation centers, colleges, and government buildings would remain closed throughout the remainder of the spring and summer, we had to pivot yet again. I realized that we had the perfect opportunity to implement PYM as a virtual program. Over the course of approximately five weeks, we made multiple adaptations to the curriculum, schedule, and research plan. We secured IRB approval for the virtual intervention; recruited and assessed youths' technology needs; ordered and distributed computer devices and individualized resilience kits to youths while adhering to the public safety mandate of masks and social distancing; and oriented the team of eleven community workers and undergraduate and graduate students who would work with us over the summer. In adapting the model for online implementation, we also changed the research methodology from a quasi-experimental study to a pre-experimental study with a pre-and post-test. This effort took an incredible amount of planning and communication, the details of which go beyond the scope of this chapter. However, we share some of our process below.

Although we were dealing with a great deal of uncertainty, the prospect of offering Project Youth MIND as virtual intervention inspired a sense of urgency in the team. We knew that youths would need constructive, safe engagement during the summer since camps and programs would not be standard in-person programming. We had regular meetings with our DCDPR partners who, along with the city government and school system, were also trying to figure out how to meet the educational, nutritional, safety, and recreation needs of our city's youths during a global pandemic. We spent hours discussing the particulars of the project, standard research procedures that became more complex, such as obtaining parental consent in the absence of a community meeting where we could answer questions and meet families. We also had to consider families who may be without a computer or who lacked technological skills to digitally sign the consent form. We made several accommodations in this area, such as allowing parents to give verbal consent by phone and texting a photo of the signed consent form for those who did not have email access. I exchanged lots of emails with parents to clarify the process and answer questions. This was indicative of the kind of flexibility we would need to have for the duration of the program. We needed to honor the fidelity of the program model but, as we soon realized, we also needed to be flexible as we were all adjusting to the new reality. Open communication and transparency with DCDPR, staff, and students helped us to stay limber. In the following sections, we share some of our insights obtained on youth engagement and program equity.

Youth Engagement

We had to balance a number of concerns to keep youths engaged in the intervention. By the time we launched PYM in late June, students had already spent several weeks completing their school year online, an abrupt change that had been thrust upon them. We managed the schedule and content delivery to avoid requiring long hours online. Daily sessions lasted from 10:00 a.m.–12:15 p.m. on Monday, Wednesday, and Thursday, with a short break in between. There was also a 45-minute, mid-week, after-lunch session so the youths could experience Hylton's Sound Vibronics music meditation session. Twice per week, youths had "Specials," a go-go music workshop (a music genre created in D.C.), and a Kemetic yoga class. The group was split by gender to promote a sense of safety and connection. We felt it was important that the intervention be meaningful and fun, maximizing the cultural expression of Black D.C. communities. With the help of a DCDPR employee, Jason Lewis, we were fortunate to have Anwan "Big G" Glover of Backyard Band, the famed D.C. go-go band, co-facilitate the go-go music workshop. Big G, also an acclaimed actor who starred in the HBO award-winning series *The Wire*, joined us every week to teach youths about music production and the history of go-go music. Many of the youths and several adults were excited to interact with Big G, who is known throughout the go-go community.

Given that we could not assemble participants for the intervention, we made arrangements to supply each participant with a PYM Resilience Kit to support their engagement in the program. The kit consisted of a yoga mat, journal, art supplies, a three-minute sand timer, a stress ball, and a tabletop chime. We coordinated with our DCDPR partners to pick up materials from UDC and distribute the kits from one of their sites at a specified time. Staff and youth safety had to be considered. For those who could not come to the distribution site, our UDC team outfitted themselves in masks and gloves, and delivered kits to students' homes. We used the materials to practice mindfulness in the virtual sessions. It was extremely gratifying to see young people using their neon green yoga mats, experimenting with the chime, and recording their thoughts in the notebooks. We often assigned them homework to teach their newly learned mindfulness skills to a family member and to practice it for a few days.

Keeping the program lively, fun, and focused was incredibly important. We delivered the 35-hour Youth MIND theme-based curriculum on restorative justice pillars, community building, nonviolent communication, mindfulness, and teen brain development using PowerPoint presentations, TEDx talks, music videos, and small group discussions and activities. We used the Zoom platform and made full use of its features to keep the sessions engaging. DCDPR site supervisor Rachelle Adkins and I.M.A.G.E. Camp director Kevin Mayo often attended the sessions. Our incredible team of 11 adults helped facilitate different program components and breakout room discussions. They brought valued expertise as probation officers, drug rehab counselors, violence interrupters, and youth workers. Some of the strategies we used to keep youth excited included a 5-minute morning stretch, "shout-outs" to acknowledge others for their effort and participation, finger snaps, upbeat music by contemporary artists, and other nonverbal ways to show support and high energy.

Joseph Green again led the spoken word segment and exposed youths to the work of poets Lucille Clifton and Patricia Smith, and other noted figures. Students were given segments of time to write as mellow hip-hop beats played in the background. Sometimes they would discuss the prompt and write in breakout rooms. Process was prioritized over progress. From the start, Green made it clear that the workshops were to inspire youths to use their voices to express their views in ways that would compel others to listen. Youths had the option of emailing their poems to Green at the end of the session. Other activities included an impromptu freestyle rap session with CashApp prizes, which was met with lots of energy. As part of the restorative circles lesson, youths created community agreements. Youth volunteers read the agreements daily to remind us of how we would engage with each other. We allowed youths to respond to discussion questions in the chat and acknowledged it as a viable way to participate, often reading aloud what they wrote; unless it was a private message, we invited them to say more about what they wrote. We regularly posted photos, videos, quotes, and mindfulness tips on the PYM Instagram page[3] as a way to stay connected to youths beyond our sessions. Our 30-minute morning staff meetings and daily debriefs following the program kept us all energized and on the same page. We shared observations of what was happening in the sessions, who was absent, or appeared distracted. We also brainstormed ideas for keeping youths engaged and tended to any scheduling needs at that time. We adapted Youth MIND in real time to respond to the needs of youths. At the end of the third week, we held a feedback session where participants assessed the program and gave us suggestions for improvement, such as reviewing the daily schedule, allowing more time for breakout groups where the students felt more comfortable talking, and reviewing the goals of the intervention so they would understand "where we are going." We promptly integrated these considerations into the project.

In a focused conversation, youths shared their thoughts on the causes of youth violence and conflict in their schools and communities. Many identified bullying, social media conflicts, gossiping, peer jealousy, and "hood beef" (rivaling neighborhoods) as the sources of fights. Several youths also acknowledged that it is not so easy to "just stop beefing" (stop arguing or fighting) with someone, and that walking away from a conflict could create the perception of cowardice. Students expressed mixed views about intervening to stop a fight. A few suggested that they

---

3. The Instagram handle for our program is @projectyouth_mind, and we encourage readers to follow us.

would try to prevent a fight by encouraging their peer to walk away or distracting them with a conversation. They also said they would remind their peer of the consequences of suspension or injury. Using restorative justice resources or school counselors to de-escalate and resolve the conflict were also among their suggestions for preventing conflict. However, they acknowledged the risks that could ensue from interfering, including getting hurt themselves or facing repercussions from school authorities; as such, many agreed it is best to "mind their business" and not get involved.

Access Is Not Equity

D.C. neighborhoods and schools are still very much segregated and we all exist within a racialized reality—dynamics that must be tended to in formal classrooms and also in virtual spaces. The PYM 2020 pilot took place during a time of intense national and global protests in response to racial violence and injustice. Issues of access and equity were also present in our daily program interactions. Unlike the 2019 group, which was comprised of all Black youths, we had five White participants in the 2020 pilot, all of whom were from more affluent sections of the city.[4] Since all youths were using videoconferencing, we were exposed to a snippet of their home lives. It was easy to notice that many young people did not have the luxury of their own room with a desk and chair (or simply chose not to use them if they did). We realized that it was a privilege for some students to be able to devote two uninterrupted hours to the program three days a week, as many were caring for young siblings and some were attending virtual summer classes. The digital divide became a salient concern as we noticed that many youths used their cell phones

---

4. We determined this using the U.S. Census zip code data.

to attend the sessions. All five of the White students (100%) appeared to participate from a secluded or semi-secluded area and used personal computers, whereas about 40% (18) used desktop computers for the sessions. Most of the Black students (60%) used the internet signal on their cell phones. Signal strength affected how quickly youths could respond to questions in online trivia games like Kahoot!, which the youths loved, and also the degree to which youths felt connected to others, since they could only see a few participants on their cell phone screens. Given these factors, we modified some of the planned curriculum activities to make them more suitable for a cell phone or tablet. Sensitive to the program's racial dynamics, it was necessary to be even more attentive to how youths participated and to remain cognizant of the subtleties of virtual engagement, such as who answered questions and how frequently, and who volunteered to serve as the breakout room speaker. These dynamics were important to monitor and to some extent, manage, to encourage equity of voice and participation in the program.

By July we were beginning to see the racial disparity in COVID-19 infections and fatalities. We did not address this explicitly in the program, yet our spoken word sessions centered on key social issues like desegregation, gentrification, police brutality, and racial identity and stereotypes. We saw ourselves as helping students manage the stress of the times by teaching them actual skills they could use in their daily lives to support their emotional well-being and providing them with a sense of connection and community. We knew that many youths came from families where adults were still working outside of the home and did not have the option of teleworking—thereby making them even more vulnerable to the virus. Youths told us they were caring for siblings and in some cases, supporting adults in their family who had fallen ill. Some were moving between the homes of parents and other loved ones, all while the pandemic was raging in the outside world.

Impact of the Intervention

A total of 46 youths enrolled in PYM, but only 34 remained on the last day of the intervention. As we had expected, there was some attrition, which resulted in fewer youths completing the post-test. We administered an exit survey that 34 youths completed. The results offer some promising data on youths' perceptions of the intervention. Of those who responded, 56% said they would continue to practice mindfulness exercises beyond the intervention. Most students indicated that the resilience kit tools they were most likely to use beyond the intervention were the stress ball (62%), the art supplies (53%), and the yoga mat (41%). The Go-Go, Teenaged Brain, Sound Vibronics, and Art workshops were those highest favored by the youths, followed by the mindfulness lessons, spoken word, and yoga activities. Youths reported their interest in learning more about some of the material covered in the program, such as Nonviolent Communication (26.5%), the Teenage Brain (20.6%), and Restorative Justice (17.6%). When asked if they would recommend the program to others, 65% said that they would. Overall, the results suggest that students liked the intervention and are interested in acquiring skills so they can better understand and express themselves and negotiate potential conflicts in peaceful ways. We also asked youths what they learned in the program. Among their responses were:

> *I learned how to communicate with others and I also learned the importance of life.*
> *I learned about the brain, resilience, and how to meditate.*

> *I learned how to take a deep breath and I learned how to calm down.*
>
> *Resilience is the ability to adapt to change.*
>
> *Stress can prevent people from doing their best, so reducing stress is important.*
>
> *I have the power to change for the better. I can express myself through writing.*
>
> *I learned different yoga positions, how to use chimes to relax, and how to do breathing exercises.*

Youths had few recommendations but offered some positive feedback, including:

> *It's cool!/It's good!/Keep doing what you're doing.*
>
> *I wish we could see each other (in person) at least once.*
>
> *Keep doing what you're doing because it makes people feel better about themselves.*
>
> *[Allow] More time with specials (music, spoken word, and yoga workshop).*

The pre- and post-tests measured change across four domains: mindfulness, handling difficult emotions, perceptions of violence, and responses to conflict. We found statistical significance in the ways students coped with emotions pre- and post-intervention, with an even greater significance among males. This suggests that the intervention may be an effective strategy for helping young people manage the complex emotions that could lead to conflict, fights, and other violent encounters among youths. Further, we found significant differences in the ways that males and females internalized and responded to anger and upset feelings, which invite a closer examination of the role of gender and socialization in violence prevention efforts.

Lessons Learned

Project Youth MIND was an eventful experience that conferred many lessons. The pilot could not have been accomplished without the devoted support of the summer program staff.[5] These individuals brought their energy and expertise to every session, offering a warm and inviting virtual community to the youth participants. The PYM summer pilot also provided a sense of purpose and predictability after three months of the stay-at-home order. The youths were endearing and energizing. At several points, the intervention felt less like research and more like a community of youths and adults coming together to offer each other mutual support during a turbulent time. We enjoyed seeing the young people's personalities emerge over the course of our weeks together. When youths were given time in the spoken word sessions to write, we also took advantage of those brief moments to pause from the constant planning, managing, and assessment. We frequently joined the yoga sessions, trying poses and participating in the guided visualizations and affirmations to support ourselves and also demystify the practices for the youths who were trying them out. In these ways, PYM supported our

---

5. The Summer 2019 PYM team consisted of Ryan Wright, Labrina Long, Sparkle Perry, Robert Rouse, and Satyani McPherson (yoga teacher) and Joseph Green and Tony Keith, Jr. (spoken word artists). The summer 2020 pilot team members were Ronald Davon Henderson, Restorative Justice & Peace Advocate with Youth and Families in Crisis, LLC; UDC undergraduate students Sparkle Perry, Okevia Pryce, and Manuel Alvarado; Norfolk State University graduate social work students Ajeenah Duncan, Miracle Hawkins, and Caitlin Seminerio. Consultants were Jason Lewis and Anwan "Big G" Glover (Go-Go music workshop), Iyelli Ichile (Kemetic Yoga instructor); Joseph Green/LMS Voice (spoken word consultant), and Ryan Wright (research consultant). K. Ivy Hylton, Founder and Executive Director, Youth and Families in Crisis, LLC, and Sharon T. Alston are co-principal investigators on Project Youth MIND and valued team members.

resilience and full presence while online. We consider it a gift to have been able to interact with the youths during the summer pilot, perhaps because it felt like such a surreal moment.

The project showed us the importance and need for spaces where youths can heal and process traumatic stress. Creating "healing spaces" within communities of color invites authentic dialogue and the ventilation of suppressed emotions. Youths are often ignored and negatively portrayed in the media, which may alienate them from larger society. Cultivating presence and empathy while with youths allows them to feel validated and understood. We suggest that adults who intend to work with youths in urban settings attune themselves to their personal biases and judgments that may help and hinder their connection with youths, consider utilizing the creative arts to reinforce cathartic expression of feelings, recruit staff members who embody the values that programs wish to reinforce, and contextualize, rather than pathologize, youth behavior.

With regard to conducting community-engaged research, teams should invest the necessary resources to cultivate familiarity, trust, and shared values among team members. This will serve as an invaluable protective factor when teams find themselves facing conflict and moments of tension, and navigating the often-choppy waves of community-engaged research. Staying nimble in response to the ever-changing dynamics of community organizations, while also remaining true to the intention of their proposed research projects, is a delicate dance—but when done well, it can yield numerous benefits.

Perhaps the greatest benefit of PYM was the space it offered youths to learn how to tend to their well-being and help manage the complexities of this moment. We were all challenged by the uncertainty that surrounded us in the summer of 2020—which also continues today. Like the youths we served, we mourned the loss of travel, vacations, D.C. street festivals, go-go band concerts, block parties, and family reunions. We missed hugging friends and loved ones and we were all were working hard to not feel so isolated and alone. With the COVID-19 pandemic still raging in 2021 at the time we are writing this chapter, in-person, end-of-year holiday and family gatherings are unlikely. Christmas, Kwanzaa, and other festivities may again be held in virtual Zoom for many families. Tending to the social emotional needs of children and youths is a major concern among educators and parents as young people struggle from the loss of in-person school interactions. Masking, social distancing, virtual schooling, and limited youth engagement continue to characterize youths' experiences in 2021. We hope that the PYM intervention offers some insight into program considerations for effectively serving our youths in this moment, especially as we continue to chart our course through a global pandemic for an unknown future.

References

Alispahic, S., & Hasanbegovic-Anic, E. (2017). Mindfulness: Age and gender differences on a Bosnian sample. *Psychological Thought*, *10*, 155–166. http://dx.doi.org/10.23668/psycharchives.1863

Ani, M. (1997). *Yurugu: An African-centered critique of European cultural thought and behavior*. All World Press.

Chatman, M. (2019). Advancing black youth justice and healing through contemplative practices and African spiritual wisdom. *Journal of Contemplative Inquiry*, 6(1), 27–46.

Corey, C., Corey, M. S., & Mutari, M. (2018). *I never knew I had a choice: Explorations in personal growth* (11th ed.). Brooks Cole.

Davis, F. E. (2019). *The little book of race and restorative justice: Black lives, healing, and U.S. social transformation*. Good Books Publishing.

Greenberg, M. T., & Harris, A. R. (2012). Nurturing mindfulness in children and youth: Current state of research. *Child Development Perspectives*, 6(2), 161–166.

Hannon, M. D., & Vereen, L. G. (2016). Irreducibility of black male clients: Considerations for competent counseling. *The Journal of Humanistic Counseling*, 55(3), 234–245. https://doi.org/10.1002/johc.12036

Jenkins, M. (2004). How do culture, class, and gender affect the practice of restorative justice? In H. Zehr & B. Toews (Eds.), *Critical issues in restorative justice* (pp. 311–323). Criminal Justice Press & Willian Publishing.

Keith, A. R. (2019). *Educational emcees: Mastering conditions in education through hip-hop and spoken words* [Doctoral dissertation, George Mason University]. Proquest.

King, R. (2018) *Mindful of race: Transforming race from the inside out*. Sounds True Inc.

Kupers, T. A. (2005). Toxic masculinity as a barrier to mental health treatment in prison. *Journal of Clinical Psychology*, 61, 713–724. https://doi.org/10.1002/jclp.20105

Ladson-Billings, G. (1995). Toward a theory of culturally relevant pedagogy. *Educational Research Journal*, 32(3), 465–491. https://doi.org/10.2307/1163320.

Love, B. L. (2016). Anti-Black state violence, classroom edition: The spirit murdering of black children. *Journal of Curriculum and Pedagogy*, 13(1), 22–25. https://doi.org/10.1080/15505170.2016.1138258

Magee, R. V. (2019). *The inner work of racial justice: Healing ourselves and transforming our communities through mindfulness*. Penguin Random House.

Morris, M. W. (2016). *Pushout: The criminalization of Black girls in schools*. The New Press.

Marasco, M. V. (2018). Addressing hegemonic masculinity with adolescent boys within the counseling relationship. *Journal of Child and Adolescent Counseling*, 4(3), 226–238. https://doi.org/10.1080/23727810.2017.1422647

Maynard, B. R., Solis, M., Miller, V., & Brendel, E. K. (2017). Mindfulness-based interventions for improving cognition, academic achievement, behavior, and socioemotional functioning of primary and secondary school students. *Campbell Systematic Reviews*. https://doi.org/10.4073/CSR.2017.5

McClaurin, I. (2001) *Black feminist anthropology: Theory, politics, praxis, and poetics*. Rutgers University Press.

Menakem, R. (2017). *My grandmother's hands: Racialized trauma and the pathway to mending our hearts and bodies*. Central Recovery Press.

Mendelson, T., & Greenberg, M. T. (2010). Feasibility and preliminary outcomes of a school-based mindfulness intervention for urban youth. *Journal of Abnormal Child Psychology*, 38(7), 985–994. https://doi.org/10.1007/s10802-010-9418-x

National Center for Education Statistics. (2015). *Indicators of school crime and safety*. U. S. Department of Education and Bureau of Justice Statistics. https://nces.ed.gov/pubs2016/2016079.pdf

Teyber, E., & Teyber, F. H. (2017). *Interpersonal process in therapy* (7th ed). Cengage Learning.

Tolan, J., & Cameron, R. (2017). *Skills in person-centered counseling & psychotherapy* (3rd ed). Sage Publishing.

Sealey-Ruiz, Y. (2007). Wrapping the curriculum around their lives: Using a culturally relevant curriculum with African American adult women. *Adult Education Quarterly 58*(1), 44–60.

Semple, R. J., Droutman, V., & Reid, B. A. (2017). Mindfulness goes to school: Things learned so far from research and real-world experiences. *Psychology in the Schools, 54,* 29–52. https://doi.org/10.1002/pits.21981

Utsey, S. O., Adams, E. P., & Bolden, M. (2000). Development and initial validation of the africultural coping systems inventory. *Journal of Black Psychology, 26*(2), 194–215. https://doi.org/10.1177/0095798400026002005

Williams, A. K., Syedullah, J., & Owens. R., L. (2016). *Radical dharma: Talking race, love, and liberation*. North Atlantic Books.

Yalom, I., & Leszcz, M. (2005). *Theory and practice of group psychotherapy* (5th ed.). Basic Books.

Yalom, I. (1980). *Existential psychotherapy*. Basic Books All World Press.

Chapter 4

Shifting the Lens from Traditional Medical Research to Fostering Community Resilience

Quianta Moore, MD, JD

This chapter pulls together my experiences as a researcher and Robert Wood Johnson Foundation Interdisciplinary Research Leaders alumn. It offers a critical and reflective approach to traditional approaches to research and offers a model to inquiry that prioritizes community engagement.

Introduction

Research can play an important role in the advancement of science, which hopefully translates into building a culture of health, as defined in the introductory chapter, for all people. The research institutions that hire and train researchers receive approximately 80% of the National Institutes of Health (NIH)'s research budget of 41 billion dollars (National Institutes of Health, 2020). Thus, research institutions have a lot of power in the allocation of those resources and play a significant role in the type of research conducted in the United States. Research is defined as "a systematic investigation, including research development, testing and evaluation, designed to develop or contribute to *generalizable* knowledge" (rule 45 CFR 46.102; Office for Research Integrity, 2022) and traditionally researchers have focused on research questions and study designs that narrowly focus on contributions to generalizable knowledge, rather than how the research benefits or harms a population or community. Yet, there is a rise in research publications describing community-engaged research and funding opportunities to support that work (Anderson et al., 2012), which can lead to stronger contributions to generalizable knowledge, as well as community benefit. Moreover, the NIH is starting to release calls for proposals that specifically focus on community-engaged research. An approach to research that integrates community members throughout the research process is called "community-based participatory research," or CBPR. CBPR is an approach to conducting research that embodies sharing power, resources, credit, results, and knowledge between communities and researchers (Wallerstein, 2003). In contrast to the traditional approach to research, this approach considers the benefits and potential harms to communities that may come from the research. The use of community-based participatory research may be an opportunity for researchers to conduct rigorous research, as well as foster community resilience.

Community resilience is an important concept in protecting and improving the health and wellbeing of communities. There are many definitions of "resilience," with origins from sociology, ecology, community development, disaster research, psychology, engineering, and many other disciplines (Norris et al., 2007). Among the different disciplines, there is not a consensus on whether resilience is an *outcome* (the ability to recover or bounce back after an adverse event), or a *process* (the ongoing act of learning and improving) (Cutter et al., 2008). Despite these differences, there is broad agreement that resilience encompasses the following capacities: absorption, adaptation, recovery, and organization (Adger et al., 2005).

The most appropriate definition for community resilience encompasses these agreed-upon capacities and emphasizes a community's ability to foster systemic change, adapt, and be proactive in response to stressors, changes, and challenges (Steiner & Markantoni, 2014). The power of community resilience lies within individual community members who collectively act to correct a problem or mitigate its impact to benefit the whole community (Houston, 2015). Because communities are made up of individuals, community and individual resilience are inextricably intertwined. A person's own resilience contributes to the overall community's resilience and adaptability (Kulig & Botey, 2016). Therefore, differences in community resilience may be related to differences in individual resilience, and efforts to increase or improve community resilience may need both individual and collective strategies.

Community resilience is important because this ability to recover from stressors contributes to neighborhood and community sustainability. Also, some communities are disproportionately impacted by adverse events, and the ability to recover is paramount in order to avoid the exacerbation of existing inequities. However, the question of what makes some communities more resilient than others remains mostly unanswered (Markantoni, Steiner, & Meador, 2019). This chapter aims to shed more light on this unanswered question by discussing the contributions of the different research approaches (traditional vs. community-based) on either hindering or fostering community resilience, and presenting a case study comparing and contrasting two similar neighborhoods, with the goal of elucidating how research can influence neighborhoods' capacity for resilience.

Power Dynamics Between Research Institutions and Communities

Research institutions like universities or federal agencies (e.g., NIH) can maintain positions of power through the allocation of resources. Access and control over resources are key components of resilience, as the capacity of a community to adapt is reliant upon where the community started before the adversity occurred. For example, if a community is well-resourced with strong social connections, the community will be in a better position to adapt, work toward systemic change, and be proactive (Markantoni, 2019). If, on the other hand, the community lacks financial resources, the baseline for the community is already at a disadvantage due to the circumstances that neighborhood disinvestment brings: poor housing, food deserts, lack of financial opportunities, and crime. Thus, the ability to "bounce back" depends on the resources to do so and a community's starting point, both collectively and individually (Markantoni, 2019).

Despite many decades of research demonstrating that lack of resources impacts health, economic opportunities and life-long trajectory, the research institution itself has not questioned how it has played a role in maintaining its own power, thereby contributing to inequity and adverse health outcomes. In 2018, $508 billion was spent on research and development in the United States (Congressional Research Service, 2020). Much of this research was human subjects research, which requires the participation of individuals. Yet, while institutions, businesses, and non-profits directly benefited from individual participation in research, most communities, especially communities of color, have not (Skloot, 2010).

Abuses of the Research Industry

Historically, research institutions have not advanced the needs or interests of the most vulnerable populations in society, nor shared the gains of research with the subjects upon whom the advancements were made. For example, in the case of Henrietta Lacks, her cells were used (without her or her family's consent) to create many medical advancements, including the polio vaccine, which have generated profits for the healthcare industry (Skloot, 2010). And yet, her family received none of the profits, nor access to these medical advancements. Given that the healthcare industry is mostly for-profit, the ability to take advantage of medical innovations is largely granted to those with the ability to pay. Research institutions benefit from federal research dollars, and use those funds to recruit and employ talented professors, expand and grow new research centers and labs, and draw top students across the country. Yet, the communities that participated in that research, without whom the research arguably could not have been conducted, receive little to no benefit.

Even more egregious is the abuse and mistreatment of people of color by a research institution. The most well-known case abuse of African Americans occurred in 1932 during the "Tuskegee Study of Untreated Syphilis in the Negro Male," where researchers intentionally misled participants with syphilis for over 40 years in order to learn about the natural progression of the disease (Centers for Disease Control, 2020). In the early 1970s, there was outcry about the inhumane and unethical treatment of African Americans during this study and it resulted in reparations for the research participants and their families (Centers for Disease Control, 2020). In the late 1970s, the Belmont Report was created, which provided guidance on the ethical conduct of research involving human subjects and laid out the following principles as foundational for research: respect for persons, beneficence, justice, and informed consent (Office of the Secretary, 1979). Later, in 1991, these ethical principles were codified in the federal statutes called the Common Rule (rule 45 CFR 46, Office for Research Integrity, 2022).

Despite the progress made in codifying rules for the ethical conduct of research, unethical research on African Americans continued. For example, in the 1990s, researchers injected African American boys, whose siblings were in the juvenile justice system, with the drug fenfluramine to determine if there was a genetic basis for aggressive or violent behavior (Washington, 2006). This study was federally funded and approved by the Institutional Review Board (IRB) at the researchers' institutions. The study was scientifically flawed, and the treatment of the children was unethical and inhumane (Washington, 2006). Fenfluramine was not approved for use in children at the time of the study, and was banned by the Food and Drug Administration in 1997 (Washington, 2006). The abuse and unethical treatment of people of color fosters mistrust of researchers and the research institution, which can create barriers to healthcare and health education, ultimately limiting individual capacity for resilience. For example, recent literature during the COVID-19 pandemic suggests that lack of trust in healthcare has contributed to disparities in COVID-19 morbidity and mortality among African Americans (Laurencin & Walker, 2020). Death and illness can reduce individual capacity to "bounce back" from other adverse events, such as police violence, loss of employment, and strained relationships, thereby limiting an individual's capacity for resilience.

Sharing Power and Research Dollars with Research Participants and Communities

Unethical and inhumane treatment of vulnerable populations by research institutions has led to an emerging field of research ethics, beyond the Belmont Report, that provides an ethical framework for guidance and interpretation of emerging issues. However, the field of ethics has not successfully moved the needle in empowering communities and sharing power. A study examining IRB reviews of research studies found that very few IRBs asked researchers about potential power imbalances between the researcher and participants (Flicker et al., 2007). Moreover, no IRB in the cited study inquired about potential community capacity-building opportunities associated with the research (Flicker et al., 2007).

In addition to the absence of encouraging researchers to be inclusive of community impact, concerns, and benefits in their work, there are also ethical principles, though well-intentioned, that have perpetuated and reinforced the power differential between the research institution and communities. For example, the topic of offering incentives for those in vulnerable populations to participate in research is debated in the literature as potentially causing an undue influence on research participation (Grant, 2004). There is a concern that if the financial incentive is high, research participants may agree to participate when they otherwise would not have, thereby compromising the consent process (Groth, 2010). Yet, there is research demonstrating that even with financial incentives, those who belong to low-income populations weigh all aspects of the risks and/or benefits of participation (Byrne, 2012). Thus, sharing grant dollars with research participants does not automatically create an undue influence.

Conversely, financial incentives and benefits for researchers are accepted without similar concerns for undue influence. For example, there are several incentives and motivating factors built into research institutions including promotion, tenure, and salary coverage, and none of these motivations are closely examined in research proposals or in granting of research dollars to research institutions. This is because benefits of conducting research—to advance and promote the institution of science—are built into the system to encourage people to enter into the field of research. While the debate over individual financial incentives will not be ended here, providing community incentives—such as jobs, opportunities to allocate grant dollars to meet community needs, and investment in capacity building for community partners—could foster resilience and create a more equitable distribution of the benefit of research participation to communities, not just research institutions. At the same time, individual participants should be compensated for the time they allocate to participating in the research, while researchers also balance ethical guidelines to protect participants from undue financial coercion or influence.

There has to be acknowledgement that communities and human subjects deserve to benefit from research beyond just altruism. Altruism does not protect individuals and communities from being exploited. In fact, research demonstrates that those who have less and those who are most vulnerable often give more (Mattis, 2009). For example, people of low income often give financially to others, even though it constitutes a great sacrifice for them (Mattis, 2009). Thus, in low-income communities the potential for abuse is greater because researchers can exploit the altruistic nature of these communities to advance their own interests, depleting the community of much-needed social capital and trust, thereby making them less resilient. The altruism of communities should not be taken advantage of—rather, it should be supported by funneling it into the creation of knowledge that could advance community well-being. Community-based participatory research aids in creating accountability for researchers to the community and can potentially decrease the risk of exploitation by ensuring community partners are part of the research process.

The practice of withholding grant dollars from communities cannot continue to be justified or considered an acceptable practice by funders and research institutions. Sharing resources is critical to advancing community resilience and the ethical principles of justice, equity, and fairness require it. In extreme cases, when the research involves a high risk of harm to research participants, there may be a legitimate concern that an extremely high incentive could be coercive, but that dilemma is solved by creating resource-sharing agreements with communities such that institutions put resources back in the community through hiring locally for research staff, supporting community businesses, and creating a pathway of opportunities for residents through educational access. Otherwise, the power dynamics between the research institutions and the public will always remain unbalanced with the greater gains favoring the institution and the greater sacrifice disadvantaging the human subject.

Likewise, a decentralization of research through the use of a CBPR approach will potentially foster shared power and resources with communities that create a collective benefit for that community. Furthermore, the concerns about incentives causing undue inducement can be mitigated by allowing community members to have more control over the research process. Shared decision-making means community members help to define research priorities, inform research practice, and provide a checks and balances system for research conducted with vulnerable populations.

There is an opportunity to create a new path forward. Often, researchers have control over the budgets submitted to funders, and have an opportunity to include an allocation of grant dollars to community partners. In fact, a great example is the Robert Wood Johnson Foundation's leadership program, Interdisciplinary Research Leaders (IRL), which requires researchers to include community partners as part of the grant.

The IRL program fosters interdisciplinary scholarship, which builds the capacity of community members and researchers to redefine research partnerships.

Although it may take longer to make institutional change in research institutions, individual researchers can forge a path that creates new standards for research that involve sharing power, resources, and decision-making. As such, researchers can help foster resilience by building community capacity to respond to change. Communities with well-established partnerships and networks are more often successful in pursuing their collective goals (Markantoni, Steiner, & Meador, 2019). Thus, community–research partnerships can support and foster community resilience through the sharing of networks and resources. In the next section, I describe my experiences with forming a community–research partnership and using a CBPR approach to research that helped to increase the resilience capacity of a community.

Putting Principles into Action: Case Study of Community-Engaged Participatory Research

The CBPR approach to research moves beyond traditional research and enables researchers to embody the principles described above and potentially foster resilience. CBPR equitably involves members of the community in the research process—specifically, those community members who the research is intended to impact. Equitable involvement means to share power, resources, and decision-making with people who may not have a background in research, nor a degree that validates their expertise. However, there is a respect and acknowledgement that community members are experts in their lived experience, history, and understanding of the challenges they face to achieve health and wellness. Additionally, community members know what strengths and opportunities can be leveraged to achieve better health outcomes. Sharing power, resources, and decision-making with community members removes the hierarchy that often exists between researchers and their human subjects. It also makes the researcher accountable to the community, rather than just accountable to a set of peers who are indoctrinated to uphold long-held beliefs about communities and maintain the status quo. Moreover, community-engaged research provides the opportunity for communities to influence what questions are being asked about them, and to drive the generation of knowledge to identify root causes and solutions to problems, rather than a constant diatribe of research that investigates their faults. Thus, this approach requires that research questions address topics of importance to the community, with the community and with the aim of combining knowledge and action for social change to improve conditions within a community.

Using a CBPR approach, our interdisciplinary research team conducted needs assessments, which we co-created with community members in two different urban, African American communities. Community members in one neighborhood (which will be called "Neighborhood A" to maintain privacy) retained their power and engaged research institutions to advance their own research priorities, while community members in the second neighborhood (noted moving forward as "Neighborhood B") experienced harm by researchers, which negatively impacted social resilience. Although the communities started at different points, this case study will demonstrate how research can help build resilience in communities.

Neighborhood A is an urban community undergoing gentrification. Neighborhood A was part of the original plans for the city, so it has been in existence for a long time, which is reflected in the community's rich history. At one time, Neighborhood A was a thriving neighborhood for upper and middle-class African-Americans. While a portion of this neighborhood is still comprised of sprawling mansions and is the home of African American professionals, people in the northern portion of the neighborhood are living in poverty. Over 65% of those who live in the northern portion of Neighborhood A make less than $20,000 a year and over 80% are renters. Yet because of its history, this community has strong interconnectedness and civic involvement. This interconnectedness and engagement were confirmed by the results of our comprehensive assessment (Moore et al., 2020). Additionally, Neighborhood A caught the attention of major philanthropic donors who made a significant $30 million investment in a historic park within the neighborhood. However, investments spurred new development in the community, and caused a domino effect of developers purchasing land in the neighborhood. Community leaders came together and engaged Massachusetts Institute of Technology (MIT) to conduct a study on how to prevent further gentrification and displacement of existing residents. Empowered with research, they then approached philanthropic organizations to partner with their community to implement the strategies recommended by MIT. A partnership ensued, and my colleagues and I were asked to conduct a comprehensive assessment of the neighborhood to identify resident needs, priorities, and strengths to inform neighborhood action.

We conducted a similar research project in Neighborhood B, which is also a predominantly African American neighborhood with a rich history and culture. However, this neighborhood was not originally part of the city, like Neighborhood A. Instead, Neighborhood B was not developed until 100 years after the creation of the city and was not annexed to the city until 50 years after neighborhood inception. Therefore, Neighborhood B started out with less city resources and investments than Neighborhood A; despite its rocky start, it still became a neighborhood of thriving businesses and abundant home ownership for African Americans in the 1960s. Currently, Neighborhood B is a mix of urban and rural houses, and is less dense than Neighborhood A. In contrast to Neighborhood A, Neighborhood B has a much higher rate of home ownership, and our needs assessment revealed that only a third of residents make less than $20,000. However, Neighborhood B has less economic diversity than Neighborhood A, and still struggles with obtaining adequate resources from the city. Neighborhood B also has strong community leadership, but it's not as broad or collective as Neighborhood A. For example, there are key leaders, such as a community-selected "Mayor" of the neighborhood who advocates for the community with the city's elected Mayor and council members to bring more resources to the neighborhood. There are also a few other leaders who work independently to try to improve the neighborhood. Prior to our project, however, they had not organized or formalized relationships amongst community leaders—nor had they effectively engaged the broader community of residents.

Project Conceptualization, Origination, and Trust-Building

Neighborhood A

The community leaders were already well organized prior to our research project. They formed a coalition of church leaders, nonprofits, business owners, and residents. They had a vision and mission for what they wanted to accomplish as a coalition and appeared to understand the value of data in advancing community priorities. For example, as described above, community leaders in Neighborhood A partnered with researchers at MIT and then engaged our research team to conduct a comprehensive assessment to identify resident priorities, needs, and neighborhood perceptions. The community coalition had predetermined priorities, a system for community engagement of residents, trust for researchers, and the capacity to engage in research.

Community leaders came to the community-based research team, which I was a part of, with specific goals in mind of the research, and wanted data on specific topics that related to the community priorities of gentrification, loss of the African American history and culture, economic mobility, and neighborhood revitalization. Health and education were not priorities, but our research team was interested in examining the relationship between resilience and health, and worked with the community leaders to agree upon the inclusion of research questions that were also important to us. We went through an iterative process in survey development with community leaders and our community researchers (described later in the chapter). We did not have to spend a lot of time building community leadership trust since they sought us out; however, we did have to earn the trust of our community researchers. Trust-building came through time; there was no magic bullet, but rather, we were consistent, transparent, and honest with the community researchers. As a result, we earned their trust over time.

Neighborhood B

The comprehensive assessment conducted in Neighborhood B was not initiated by the community. Rather, the research team conceptualized the idea and reached out to community partners to gauge interest. We obtained buy-in with a local nonprofit that provided direct services near the neighborhood, and partnered with that nonprofit to collaborate on the research project. We set forth roles and responsibilities at the outset and made sure we had a research plan that supported shared decision-making and resource allocation. Our community partner had little experience with community engagement, and had not established trust with community leaders and residents. Therefore, our community–research partnership in Neighborhood B required that we establish trust with grassroots leaders and create a mechanism for research oversight by the community. We ultimately established a Community Advisory Board (CAB) with grassroots leaders, but it took several months of meeting with individual leaders, attending community events, and relationship and trust-building. They had to get to know us—not just as researchers, but also as people. They asked questions about our personal lives, our faith, and our track record working with communities.

One of the main reasons for the lack of trust in Neighborhood B was the community's prior experience with researchers. During our initial meeting with community leaders, they described prior research studies where they "partnered" with researchers to conduct research in their neighborhood, only to have the researchers not share the data and/or only report negative findings. In several community conversations, community members talked about researchers in the late 1980s during the HIV epidemic who then released the data to the media. These data shed a negative light on the community as being a hotspot for HIV. They described the harms to the community that resulted from the researcher's actions: people moved out of the neighborhood, important social connections were broken, and access to resources became limited. The neighborhood became stigmatized, resulting in a decline in community resilience.

Even though this event happened 40 years ago, community members recounted the events as if they happened yesterday, and the feelings of betrayal and harm were still fresh. The negative experience of this community is not unlike communities all across the nation who report similar harms of researchers releasing sensitive data that led to stigmatization of their communities (Flicker et al., 2007). Although public health researchers may have valid, scientific reasons for determining disease "hotspots," how that data are communicated and used should be done in partnerships with communities so as to not eliminate trust. Research-inflicted harm in Neighborhood B created a barrier to participation in neighborhood-wide initiatives, which limited additional neighborhood resources, resulting in a stagnation of resilience. Moreover, negative perceptions about community resilience and social cohesion in Neighborhood B were held by local philanthropy and policymakers due to the lack of participation of community members in funded efforts to improve neighborhood conditions, creating a cycle of reinforcement of lack of trust and disinvestment in the community.

To gain community leader trust in Neighborhood B, we established clear guidelines for our partnership, which held us accountable to the community leaders forming the community advisory board. We compensated the community leaders $500 each for their participation in a total of six meetings held over the course of the year. This small compensation for the leaders' time represented a huge step toward demonstrating that we were committed to valuing their participation. Further, we supported them in creating a common branding for their collective work to increase resident awareness of the CAB's efforts.

Resident Trust of Community Partners and Its Impact on Research

Individual resilience is an important component of community resilience. Therefore, fully exploring and understanding the relationship between the myriad roles of community partners and how they engage with community residents is critical in fostering community resilience. In Neighborhood A, the community partners who solicited the research were part of organizations that regularly engaged community residents and were trusted by fellow community organizations. On the other hand, there was a paucity of organizations who served Neighborhood B, and our community partner was not an organization that was well respected by neighborhood residents. The lack of trust was not a consequence of maleficence by our community partner, but rather a lack of experience in authentic community engagement that went beyond the traditional service delivery model. During the course of our research project, our community partner also increased its organizational capacity to engage with community residents in ways that build trust and resilience.

Because we understood that there could be varying levels of trust of community organizations, our research team wanted to develop relationships with residents in both communities and not rely solely on the community organizations to interface with residents. We felt this was important to demonstrate our respect for resident participation in the research as well as offering our expertise to be thought partners in translating the research into actionable steps. In both Neighborhoods A and B, we held several meetings with residents to communicate research findings, and we worked with community residents to create infographics and other products to visualize the data in a simple, useful way. Further, in both communities, our community partners organized interested residents into workgroups based on priorities that arose from the data, and continued to meet and work with residents to develop strategies.

Another key component of our research process was sharing decision-making. For example, in Neighborhood A, the community members drove the research process and decided there was no need to establish an additional CAB to participate in the decision-making process. However, a CAB was necessary in Neighborhood B because there were no pre-existing community priorities and strategies in place that defined the scope of the research. The CAB was equally involved in every decision made throughout the research process.

Fostering Resilience Through Community-based Participatory Research

A core principle of CBPR is the decentralization of the research process, and as such we shared grant dollars, decision-making, and research priorities with community members. In both Neighborhoods A and B, we made an intentional effort to invest in neighborhood residents and local businesses. We hired residents as community researchers and paid them $15/hour for approximately 30–40 hours per week over the grant period to assist with community engagement, administer the survey, and inform research activities. This helped to increase quality of living for residents—some moved into new housing and purchased cars—which increased individual capacity to engage in advocacy efforts within the community (thereby contributing to community resilience). We intentionally recruited residents who had difficulty obtaining traditional employment because of criminal records, being out of the labor market for a long time, or not having requisite "soft skills." We developed a robust training program and partnered with local organizations to provide our community researchers with additional job training support. We hired a former community organizer to manage the community researchers and survey administration in both neighborhoods. We also purchased all of our supplies and food from businesses in the community to increase revenue in the neighborhood. Lastly, we compensated research participants $50 for their time completing the survey. Who we hired and how we allocated grant resources were critical in developing community respect and trust for our team in both neighborhoods. Our research approach (e.g., paying people a living wage) contributed to the opportunities for individuals to build resilience because our community researchers were able to acquire better housing and transportation, and ultimately secure long-term employment after the projects were completed.

The research questions and survey were co-developed with community partners and residents. In Neighborhood A, the process was more community driven since leaders already had ideas about what information they wanted captured. In Neighborhood B, we started with a list of potential survey domains and the CAB selected the topics of greatest importance to their neighborhood (based on their experience and perspectives). Transparent and honest communication throughout the research process is vital to building and maintaining trust with the community, and it also helps to avoid problems later on. In both neighborhoods, we listened to community priorities and also communicated that there were certain topics of interest that were important to the research team. We agreed upon survey domains that were important to community members, as well as topics that were of interest to our team. We also prioritized questions pertaining to community strengths and assets because the narrative surrounding communities of color is often negative, fueled by research that consistently highlights deficits in minority neighborhoods, especially in African American communities. But often, based on a review of many survey instruments and over a decade of experience conducting and reviewing research, the reason the findings are only correlated with negative factors is because those were the only questions asked. Contrarily, we wanted our research to investigate community strengths that could be leveraged to enhance neighborhood health and wellbeing and mitigate adverse outcomes, as well as contribute to the understanding of resilience. We wanted to shift this paradigm and explore a factor that seemed to be related to community resilience: prosocial behaviors. Prosocial behaviors are actions intended to help or benefit another individual or group of individuals (Eisenberg & Mussen, 1989), and are associated with increased individual resilience (Haroz et al., 2013). This decision to focus on understanding the strengths in the community and how those could be optimized and leveraged to improve community health led to interesting research findings, and opportunities for the community to change the narratives about their neighborhood. Ultimately, in Neighborhood A, our research contributed to nonprofits shifting priorities to better serve the community and community organizations obtaining additional funding. Together, these results increased community capacity and resilience. In Neighborhood B, CAB members used the research to apply for another grant, which they received.

Resilience Outcomes for the Neighborhoods

The neighborhoods started at different levels of resilience and capacity, and therefore our investment in the neighborhoods had differing degrees of impact. There are several key insights about Neighborhood A that demonstrate community resilience. Although the community had several pre-existing challenges, such as lack of economic opportunities and inadequate housing, the new challenge of gentrification was met with all of the characteristics of resilience: proactivity, willingness to engage in systemic change, and adaptation. Community organizations and individuals proactively engaged researchers to obtain needed data to present to philanthropy; developed data-informed strategies to mitigate the impact of new development on resident displacement; and adapted continually to new information, new circumstances, and new challenges throughout the engagement process. In Neighborhood A, community organizations were able to leverage our research to influence policymakers, apply for additional funding, and use it as opportunities to engage neighborhood residents in the data to demonstrate common concerns and strengths. Moreover, individual resilience was supported through resident engagement efforts by community leaders to address identified needs, connect residents with initiatives in the community, and create jobs through our grant.

On the other hand, Neighborhood B started with several challenges to overcome and had a lower initial capacity to take advantage of the research project to advance community interests. The individual community leaders who formed our CAB in Neighborhood B never worked together prior to our project, and there was not an existing network of community organizations that could support a community-wide effort. Our research team and community partner worked with CAB members to develop messaging to increase neighborhood awareness of their existence, purpose, and opportunities to get involved. We also facilitated a community meeting that was hosted by CAB members to share survey findings with residents and various community stakeholders. We invested a lot of time in supporting the CAB in ways that didn't directly relate to conducting the research, but our efforts helped to build the community's capacity to use research findings at the conclusion of the study. Moreover, several of the members formalized their partnership by obtaining 501(c)(3) status and our community partner continued to work with CAB members to use data to drive change in the neighborhood. Thus, despite challenges in Neighborhood B, our research project was able to support the formation of a nonprofit that subsequently received grant dollars, the community gained positive media coverage of neighborhood strengths, and the experience fostered an increased trust in researchers (as reported by CAB members). We also contributed to individual resilience in creating new job opportunities for residents and brokering trust in our community partner, which will facilitate increased services in the community.

Of note, an important component of continued support for community proactivity and agency is sharing data ownership with community organizations and establishing agreed-upon data usage and access parameters that give community members access to data to advance community interests. A major grievance from communities and organizations regarding the conduct of researchers is not making research findings and data available to community members. A mechanism for community organizations to have continued access to data should be established early and submitted to the IRB to avoid issues at the end of the project, which could erode the trust built early on.

These research projects are an example of equitable research that contributes to building and supporting resilience in both individuals and communities. More than the research itself, how the research is conducted and how resources are allocated can have long-lasting impacts on individuals and communities, thereby fostering resilience. Communities' agency and receptivity to change can be fostered through the research process, which positions communities to attract additional resources even after the project is long completed. For example, during the COVID-19 pandemic, funders asked which communities had organizational capacity to receive grant dollars. Previously in Neighborhood B, community members worked independently with no formalized structure. Now, they had the capacity to receive grant dollars after formalizing their organization into a redevelopment corporation. In this way, our project helped to position the neighborhood to apply for and be a recipient of support during the pandemic. Additionally, literature demonstrated that project success can help to build resilience (Markantoni, Steiner,

& Meador, 2019). Therefore, the successful completion of both projects helped to foster resilience in both neighborhoods.

Project Takeaways

Neighborhoods A and B started out with different levels of capacity for resilience. Our assessment identified several characteristics of Neighborhood A that support resilience, including high levels of prosocial behavior, knowledge and experience of coalition-building, resident engagement, and comfort and understanding of the value of research and data. On the other hand, the assessment of Neighborhood B identified fewer factors that could support resilience (i.e., no formalized community leader structure, less perceived community resilience by funders, and mistrust of the research process). Yet, CBPR principles created an opportunity for Neighborhood B to increase the factors of resilience and develop agency and capacity to achieve common goals. The CAB continued to exist beyond the research project, which creates opportunities for continued momentum in the neighborhood, as well as the leaders' ability to collectively respond to neighborhood adversities. Thus, even though the neighborhoods started out with vastly different experiences with researchers and data, we believe our project helped to reestablish some trust in research and created an opportunity for community leaders to see the value of data.

Lessons Learned

What's the real purpose of research? We posit that research has to move from just advancing knowledge to advancing empowerment. It is not sufficient for researchers to only contribute to the advancement of their respective disciplines, with no contribution to the individuals and communities that helped them advance the research institution. There is a well-established system that promotes and maintains the status quo of research institutions, which may be difficult to change overnight. However, there is an increasing value and recognition of CBPR by the National Institutes of Health, Centers for Disease Control, and many other philanthropic foundations, such as the Robert Wood Johnson Foundation. This recognition gives researchers the opportunity and financial support to reshape how research is conducted; specifically for the author of this chapter and the project research team, we are able to apply the principles described in this chapter to our research. Yet, researchers may still feel pressure from their research institutions to conform to traditional research approaches. Thus, more work is required to shift the values and priorities of research and academic institutions toward a more community-oriented research approach.

Researchers who want to replicate our model should use the following strategies: 1) Involve both community leaders and residents in the entire research process, from conception to design, analysis, and interpretation of results; this may require budgeting for additional time for the researcher and staff to attend community meetings and other trust-building activities; 2) allocate grant dollars fairly and compensate community members for their involvement in the research; 3) identify opportunities to invest in the neighborhood by supporting local businesses when purchasing research supplies and/or employing residents; 4) help to support community usage of data and information to advance community interests; and 5) allow community members to review research products (i.e., manuscripts, policy papers, etc.) prior to dissemination.

This is a more time-intensive research approach, and it does not come without sacrifice. But the opportunity to positively impact communities and foster resilience is worth the sacrifice, and increases the value and contribution of research to society. Moreover, the proposed approach to research has the potential to build a culture of health grounded in equity, justice, and self-determination for all.

References

Adger, W. N., Arnell, N. W., & Tompkins, E. L. (2005). Successful adaptation to climate change across scales. *Global Environmental Change, 15*(2), 77–86.

Anderson, E. E, Solomon, S., Heitman, E., DuBois, J. M., Fisher, C. B., Kost, R. G., Lawless, M. E., Ramsey C, Jones B, Ammerman A, & Friedman Ross, L. (2012). Research ethics education for community-engaged research: A review and research agenda. *Journal of Empirical Research on Human Research Ethics, 7*(2), 3–19.

Braveman, P., & Gottlieb, L. (2014). The social determinants of health: It's time to consider the causes of the causes. *Public Health Reports, 129*(2), 19–31. https://doi.org/10.1177/00333549141291S206

Byrne, M. M., Croft, J. R., French, M. T., Dugosh, K. L, & Frestinger, D. S. (2012). Development and preliminary results of the Financial Incentive Coercion Assessment Questionnaire. *Journal of Substance Abuse Treatment, 43*, 86–93.

Centers for Disease Control. (2020). *U.S. Public Health Service syphilis study at Tuskegee: The Tuskegee timeline.* https://www.cdc.gov/tuskegee/timeline.htm

Congressional Research Service. (2020, Jan 24). *U.S. research and development funding and performance: Fact sheet.* https://fas.org/sgp/crs/misc/R44307.pdf

Cutter, S. L., Barnes, L., Berry, M., Burton C., Evans, E., Tate, E., & Webb, J. (2008). A place-based model for understanding community resilience to natural disasters. *Global Environmental Change, 18*(4), 598–606.

Eisenberg, N., & Mussen, P. H. (1989). The roots of prosocial behavior in children. New York: Wiley. http://dx.doi.org/10.1017/CBO9780511571121

Flicker, S., Travers R., Guta A., McDonald S., & Meagher, A. (2007). Ethical dilemmas in community-based participatory research: Recommendations for

Institutional Review Boards. *Journal of Urban Health: Bulletin of the New York Academy*, *84*(4), 478–493.

Grant, R.W., & Sugarman, J. (2004). Ethics in human subjects research: Do incentives matter? *Journal of Medicine and Philosophy*, *29*(6), 717–738.

Groth, S.W. (2010). Honorarium or coercion: Use of incentives for participation in clinical research. *Journal of the New York State Nurses Association*, *41*(1), 11–22.

Haroz, E. E., Murray, L. K., Bolton, P., Betancourt, T., & Bass, J. K. (2013). Adolescent resilience in Northern Uganda: The role of social support and prosocial behavior in reducing mental health problems. *Journal on Research in Adolescence*, *23*(1), 138–148.

Houston, J. B. (2015). Bouncing forward: Assessing advances in community resilience assessment, intervention, and theory to guide future work. *American Behavioral Scientist*, *59*(2), 175–180.

Kulig, J., & Botey, A. P. (2016). Facing a wildfire: What did we learn about individual and community resilience? *Natural Hazards*, 82, 1919–1929.

Laurencin, C. T., & Walker, J. M. (2020). A pandemic on a pandemic: Racism and Covid-19 in Blacks. *Cell Systems*, *11*, 9–10.

Markantoni, M., Steiner, A. A., & Meador, J. E. (2019). Can community interventions change resilience? Fostering perceptions of individual and community resilience in rural places. *Community Development*, *50*(92), 238–255.

Mattis, J. S., Hammond, W. P., Grayman, N., Bonacci, M., Brennan, W., Cowie, S.-A., Ladyzhenskaya, L., & So, S. (2009). The social production of altruism: Motivations for caring action in a low-income urban community. *American Journal of Community Psychology*, *43*, 71–84.

Moore, Q. L., Kulesza, C., Kimbro, R., Flores, D., & Jackson, F. (2020). The role of pro-social behavior in promoting physical activity, as an indicator of resilience, in a low-income neighborhood. *Behavioral Medicine*, *46*(3–4), 353–365.

National Institutes of Health: Budget. (2020.) https://www.nih.gov/about-nih/what-we-do/budget

Norris, F. H., Stevens, S. P., Pfefferbaum, B., Wyche, K. F., & Pfefferbaum, R. L. (2007). Community resilience as a metaphor, theory, set of capacities, and strategy for disaster readiness. *American Journal of Community Psychology*, *41*, 127–150.

Office for Research Integrity (2022). 45 CFR 46. https://ori.hhs.gov/content/chapter-3-The-Protection-of-Human-Subjects-45-crf-46102-protection-human-subjects

Office of the Secretary. (1979). *The Belmont report: Ethical principles and guidelines for the protection of human subjects of research.* The National Commission for the Protection of Human Subjects of Biomedical and Behavioral Research. https://www.hhs.gov/ohrp/regulations-and-policy/belmont-report/read-the-belmont-report/index.html

Skloot, R. (2019). *Immortal life of Henrietta Lacks.* New York Crown Publishers.

Steiner, A., & Markantoni, M. (2014). Exploring community resilience in Scotland through capacity for change. *Community Development Journal, 49,* 407–425. https://doi.org/10.1093/cdj/bsto42

Wallerstein, N., & Duran, B. (2003). The conceptual, historical and practical roots of community based participatory research and related participatory traditions. In M. Minkler & N. Wallerstein (Eds.), *Community-based participatory research for health* (pp. 27–52). Jossey-Bass.

Washington, H. (2006). *Medical apartheid: The dark history of medical experimentation on Black Americans from the colonial times to the present.* Harlem Moon.

Chapter 5

The Resilience Dilemma

Jomo Kheru

This chapter examines and critiques the construct of resilience from an African-centered perspective. The discussion and recommendations outlined in this chapter were formed through experiences living and working in my community and through research conducted as a research scholar in the Robert Wood Johnson Foundation leadership program, Interdisciplinary Research Leaders.

We stuck in La-La Land; Even when we win, we gon' lose. —JAY-Z

From an African-centered perspective, resilience is an awkward, difficult term to deal with, for at least two reasons. First, it focuses attention on the marginalized individuals in society, and essentially puts a "burden of proof" on them to demonstrate their value, merit, or abilities. This has been especially true in the context of education research, and reflects the racialized, gendered society that supports it. Specifically, the Eurocentric, patriarchal norms of American culture tend to create environments where the victims are themselves blamed for their victimization. They are then forced to overcome or excel, or otherwise *will* themselves out of a predicament in which they never should have been placed in the first place. This "will" construct, expressed in various contexts (e.g., individual, family, community, clinical, educational) has come to be referred to as "resilience" (Brown, 2006; Masten, 2018; Van Breda, 2001). Secondly, resilience research largely reflects and gives rise to hegemony in Western/ European society itself through the unspoken and clear power dynamics that it generates between researchers and participants; funding agencies, institutions, and researchers; and even researchers themselves.

This chapter approaches the construct of resilience from a perspective that prioritizes the histories, lived experiences, and future possibilities of African people. It also offers researchers interested in solutions to social, economic, and political systems assaulting Black community health four practical recommendations borne out of my limited experiences working in the field, as well as my journey as a scholar-intellectual. Ultimately, this chapter represents a call for a decolonized research methodology (Chilisa, 2019; Smith, 2013).

My First Time

Although I started my research career in earnest as a graduate student, my first exposure to research activity was as an undergraduate psychology major. My experimental psychology professor mentored me as I co-presented a paper on involuntary leg movement research he had conducted at the Imhotep Student Interdisciplinary Research Conference. This was 1999. I remember barely even understanding the point of what we were trying to accomplish, both from a methodological standpoint with the study, and from a functional standpoint with the conference presentation.

I was a Black kid from poor neighborhoods and "failing" public schools. The oldest of five, I was the first from my family (on both sides) to go to college. I earned good grades and worked hard—facts that I attribute to my parents. I was smart—most of school came easy to me. Twenty years later, I've conducted and presented more research than I can remember. A good deal of it has involved community spaces in education; this is a fact that reflects my own intentionality and agency as a researcher. In other words, now I choose my research endeavors and activities.

Or do I?

Here we hear the first whispers of the resilience dilemma. If we listen closely, we can hear the version of my educational journey that warms our hearts, makes us smile, and gives us optimism. In this version, the narrative focuses on how much *I've* overcome—the obstacles that *I* avoided; the identity that *I* constructed; the supports that *I* benefited from. The dangers and pitfalls associated with growing up Black and poor are cast as the villains in my triumphant tale of academic achievement and educational attainment. After all, I went on to earn a doctorate, and as a faculty member, I now function as part of the very system that has represented the villains in my own story. Awards, certificates, grants, degrees, fellowships, stipends, publications, and recognition ... all of these are the rewards for possessing that "special something" that allowed *me* to succeed.

Because so many others have failed.

The Dark Side

Legendary basketball coach Mike Krzyzewski was once quoted as saying, "Imagination has a great deal to do with winning."[1] I imagine that he was referring to the importance of imagining oneself as a winner en route to actually making it happen. However, like my own personal story there is another way to interpret Coach K's statement.

If we consider "winning" as a construct, then Coach K's statement takes on new meaning. Perhaps what he meant was something closer to: "Winning isn't real; one has to use their imagination in order to see it." It is easy to take the existence of winners and losers for granted; after all, we receive countless messages to reinforce this conditioning on a day-to-day—and in some cases, hour-to-hour—basis for most of our lives. Competition, we are taught, is part of human nature; in fact, according to Darwin (1909), it is part of nature itself. The proverbial goal, then, is to win at the game of life. Those who win, celebrate. Those who don't win, try again: *Resilience*.

Let us look momentarily at the losers. Who are they? What are their characteristics? Where are they from? How many of them are there? In a system where everyone is either a winner or loser, the construct of resilience sounds a lot like Coach K's imagination—imagining that you're a winner (when you're really not) and perhaps even imagining that there really are winners and losers in the first place.

The sports world illustrates both types of imaginings. During his nearly 20-year career, NBA superstar Kobe Bryant hit 36 game-winning shots.[2] Each time, fans watching across the country (and the world)

---

1. https://ftw.usatoday.com/2016/02/best-sports-quotes-about-winning
2. https://fadeawayworld.com/2016/06/29/kobe-bryants-all-game-winners-of-his-career-36/

cheered and celebrated as if Bryant's win was their win, too. This is fascinating because (gambling scenarios aside) Bryant's efforts and outcomes had no effect whatsoever on the lives of these fans. From one standpoint, Bryant's fans imagined that they were winners, thereby enabling their own personal celebration and elation in the absence of any material connection to Bryant whatsoever.

To see the second, more profound type of imagining, all we need to do is examine the losers. Each of Bryant's 36 game-winning shots made him a winner, both in those moments and the context of those games, and in the long-term sense. Bryant's enduring legacy is one of a winner—not just as a player, but as a father, a mentor, and a leader. But each of Bryant's 36 game-winning shots also generated a loser. Again, I ask: Who are *they*?

Part of the reason why resilience is an awkward construct from an African-centered perspective is because it essentially prevents us from asking this question. Losing isn't seen as a trait, it's seen as a state—a temporary, if unfortunate holding place for eventual winners. "Losing" simply becomes "pre-winning." In a world of new and "pre-owned" cars, resilience helps make sure that nobody feels used.

Not Equal

Just as losing is seen as pre-winning, African people in America have been seen as existing on an evolutionary trajectory towards Whiteness. For hundreds of years, African people have been seen as (and as a result, have come to see ourselves as) pre-White. Caught in a multigenerational spin cycle of trying to get clean, African people in America have endured the cultural rape, theft, and debasement of entire systems of White supremacy in an effort to finally "win." From a media perspective, in the 1970s, *The Jeffersons* exemplified "movin' on up." In the 1990s, the Huxtables proved that the Black family could live and behave like the White family. In the 2000s, we've seen an explosion of Black celebrities via entertainment and social media that transcend barriers of poverty and live carefree, lavish, indulgent lifestyles. Similarly, in education, we've witnessed cultural monism on an increasing scale—almost universally, European-centered education has been the norm for Black and Brown students since this country's inception. According to Carruthers (1999):

> Today, science education ignores the fact that the Ancient Egyptians were considered by individuals such as Aristotle and Francis Bacon to be the founders of mathematics and certain sciences. Ignoring the Egyptian mathematical and medical texts, while still explaining the impact of Euclid and Pythagoras on geometry, is a clear case of unacceptable Eurocentrism. Highlighting the Hippocratic Oath, while ignoring the medicine and surgery of the ancient Egyptians, is yet another example. In fact, one can take science and mathematics from elementary school through the Ph.D. degree and never learn that a single African contributed one idea to either science of mathematics. (p. 97)

Resilience, then, becomes that quality, which enables African people to endure. After all, it's a tough road.

Traveling this road is so tough, in fact, that many educational researchers and scholars have begun to study the "trauma" resulting from navigating it. Racial trauma in education is generally discussed as negative psychosocial or clinical effects of discrimination or harassment due to racism. Much of the work in this field centers on the development of assessment models and treatment interventions that incorporate the experiences of Black students and educators (Jernigan & Daniel, 2011).

What both resilience and trauma studies almost completely tend to omit is the reality that African people and culture both pre-date and continue to exist *outside* of the parameters of Euro-American paradigms and frameworks. In other words, Blackness and the experiences of people of African descent cannot be described as resulting from European cultural patterns or by our intersections with systems of European domination, colonialism, and White supremacy.

My own personal story then, can be told without reference to those systemic obstacles that were placed in my way on the road to academic achievement and success. It should be told without the chauvinistic assumption that my goals, destinies, and purposes as an African man and intellectual and father and brother and teacher and son can be defined by diplomas and tenure and promotion. It should not be told as if I have had any real self-determination in my decisions and educational opportunities; as with the conveyor belt often described in high school prep and college athletics en route to the professional ranks (Rhoden, 2010), these were carefully laid out for me at each stage. Mine is not a story of resilience; mine is a story of violation. I was denied my ancestors' rich legacy (James, 1954) of spirituality, medicine, astronomy, art, technology, literature, science, and philosophy. Thousands of years of human accomplishment and failure were erased, rewritten, and then used to justify a disparaged 500 years of chattel slavery and *Maafa* (Ani, 1994).

In a critical chapter titled "The Eschatological Dilemma: The Problem of Studying the Black Male Only as the Deaths That Result from Anti-Black Racism," Curry (2015) wrote:

> The sensibilities of the Black American intellectual concerning race have historically been cemented to their ascendency within empire. How one writes about race, offering hope for change in opposition to the totality of racism, and communicates an aspiration for

> the possibilities made available by American ideas like freedom, justice and equality has separated the radical from the progressive. In "The Failure of the Black Intellectual," E. Franklin Frazier describes Black intellectualization as de-niggerization of Black scholarship, a retreat from using Black experience as the foundation of theorizing the Blackness, or an "emptying of his [her] life of meaningful and content and ridding him of all Negro identification." The study of Black folk under the integrationist milieu shows the danger Black intellectuals, the Black bourgeoisie pose to our conceptualizations of our thinking about Blackness, which was described by Carter G. Woodson's *Miseducation of the Negro* (1933). In trying to distort the content of Blackness to fit within the confines of disciplinary study, the study of Black folk by the academic class simultaneously reflects the desire of the Black intellectual to be the beneficiary of anthropological histories/post-racial possibilities of white humanity, while separating themselves as a class from the pathological representation(s) associated with the Nigger which inhibit their transcendence. Assimilating canonical knowledge(s) then acts as the means by which life is grasped—revelation, pulling the Black intellectual away from the wretchedness sown into the flesh of Black people and the death of Niggers. (p. 479)

Curry's point here is clear: that the only goals of the Black intellectual who uses European cultural frameworks to describe Black folk are assimilation and ascendency within the very system responsible for our collective demise. This is not me, and that is not my story.

Thus, my offering to those interested in community-engaged research is that of Robert Williams (1974) who, in an article titled "The Death of White Research in the Black Community," warned us with the ancient African proverb, "Never let the fox in the henhouse to feed the chickens" (p. 116).

With that warning safely under our arms, let us examine lessons learned from educational settings that focus on how to prevent Eurocentrism from creating division and apathy, and ultimately undermining authentic efforts on the part of researchers interested in community engagement. In my experience, educational interventions and pedagogy often serve as the basis for community-engaged work—either directly through efforts to help disenfranchised Black and Brown students negotiate their schoolwork, or indirectly through what I refer to as the "carryover effect." The carryover effect is the intangible but real influence that Eurocentric educational practices have on Black children who lack an African cultural sensibility. Such children are psychologically defenseless against the classic forms of racial attack from teachers and peers (e.g., discrimination and harassment); but more importantly, they are confused into a blithering sort of internal turmoil, puzzlement, and uncertainty about life and their roles in it. James Baldwin (1965) captured this phenomenon:

> On the other hand, I have to speak as one of the people who have been most attacked by the Western system of reality. It comes from Europe. That is how it got to America. It raises the question of whether or not civilizations can be considered equal, or whether one civilization has a right to subjugate—in fact, to destroy—another.
>
> Now, leaving aside all the physical factors one can quote—leaving aside the rape or murder, leaving aside the bloody catalogue of oppression which we are too familiar with any way—what the system does to the subjugated is to destroy his sense of reality. It destroys his father's authority over him. His father can no longer tell him anything because his past has disappeared.
>
> In the case of the American Negro, from the moment you are born every stick and stone, every face, is white. Since you have

> not yet seen a mirror, you suppose you are, too. It comes as a great shock around the age of 5, 6, or 7 to discover that the flag to which you have pledged allegiance, along with everybody else, has not pledged allegiance to you. It comes as a great shock to see Gary Cooper killing off the Indians, and although you are rooting for Gary Cooper, that the Indians are *you*. (emphasis added, p. 32)

With these words in mind, I'll outline several recommendations for engaged researchers.

Recommendations for Decolonizing Research

Following are four recommendations for researchers interested in decolonizing research practices to avoid the resilience dilemma, which is the tendency to identify, define, and even celebrate Black folks' abilities to survive in the face of challenge and adversity.

Recommendation #1

I find it necessary to plainly identify researchers for who they are—well-intentioned but ultimately nefarious agents whose funding and resources ought not be confused with friendship and trust. Therefore, it is important that researchers recognize the constraints and limits of the researcher–community relationship and use clear, open communication about decisions, processes, and goals. This will enable researchers to allow community stakeholders to function with clarity and dignity in the context of the research. One approach to help facilitate discussions around community and organization priorities and communication is through the Facilitated Community Dialogues Initiative.

Facilitated Community

The Facilitated Community Dialogues Initiative (FCDI) is a project of the Tides Center funded by the Robert Wood Johnson Foundation, designed to strengthen understandings about community leadership through shared learning experiences between people fostering health equity through institutions that research, fund, and deliver programs to impact the social determinants of health (e.g., foundations, universities, and clinical and public health agencies) and community leaders with direct lived experience grappling with and challenging health inequities. FCDI is currently working with a growing network of local nonprofit community-based organizations working to solve problems in the areas of public health and education. These organizations serve in a variety of backgrounds and applied disciplines, including food safety and sustainability, faith-based ministry, youth development, crisis support, housing, violence prevention, and workforce development.

FCDI has partnered with organizations from across the country to engage their communities using the Structured Dialogue method or SDM, which is discussed in detail in the second recommendation. These organizations are working with communities most impacted by inequalities to address the root causes of inequities (e.g., ideas, values, strategies) impacting the community. The goal of the FCDI partnership is to help community organizations gain a greater understanding about what is and isn't working in their approaches to enhance both community self-determination and agency to take action.

Although each organization is unique, a few patterns have emerged with respect to the organization's engagement with SDM. First, several organizations have valued SDM for its potential to facilitate internal organizational decision-making, which helps during research engagement. Challenges and obstacles to effective organizational decision-making are a proven key factor in the success of community organizations (Hopkins, Meyer, Shera, & Peters, 2014; Louis, 2006; Parker, 2004) and it is crucial that leadership be able to plan and strategize at high levels. Because it incorporates and encourages disagreement between stakeholders in ways that benefits the group, various levels of leadership (e.g., volunteers, staff, program directors) tend to share their experiences in ways that individuals with other roles can appreciate and understand.

Recommendation #2

Encourage research participants to talk with each other. Make every effort to create space for them to share their ideas and feelings with others. Consider creating time and space for them to meet privately without researchers present in order to strategize and team-build, recognizing that the potential benefits of the research only exist at the community (not individual) level.

The Structured Dialogue Method (SDM)

The SDM is an innovative, engaging, culturally responsive communication platform designed to enhance higher-level critical thinking and analytical skills in a variety of community and educational contexts. The SDM is situated within several ancient African and contemporary African American cultural traditions of oral communication and has been studied in a variety of educational contexts with African American students, including K–12 STEM education, undergraduate course design, and community settings in the U.S. and abroad.

Freire (1970) outlined *dialogue* as a liberation modality that can be used as pedagogy in the college classroom. According to Freire, "dialogue" is defined as "an encounter between men, mediated by the world, in order to name the world" (p. 69). Students become active participants not in the curriculum, but in their own personal and intellectual transformation. In this model, students create (develop) their own ideas about course material. Freire explained:

> Finally, true dialogue cannot exist unless the dialoguers engage in critical thinking—thinking which discerns an indivisible solidarity between the world and the people and admits of no dichotomy between them—thought which perceives reality as process, as transformation, rather than as a static entity—thinking which does not separate itself from action, but constantly immerses itself in temporality without fear of the risks involved. (p. 92)

Actualizing dialogue given the aforementioned constraints imposed by an oppressive pedagogical, curricular, and informational structure calls for a model that is flexible enough to adapt to widely variant classroom and educational contexts, but cohesive enough to frame the activities of instructors and students in liberatory (as opposed to oppressive) practices.

Structured dialogue offers a way for individuals to engage one another and material critically and purposefully toward mutual growth. Structured dialogue has been conceptualized in various ways in the educational literature, all of them focusing on the iterative, progressive construction of perspective through the vulnerable exchange of ideas between equal participants (Boyd, 2008; Burkhart & Limaye, 2008; Shumway, 1989; Sleeter, 1996; Vella, 2008). The SDM allows students to initiate and participate in a series of dialogues focusing on course material and provides instructors with valid tools and skill sets for informal and formal assessment. The SDM encompasses four stages, and is summarized as follows:

Stage 1: The instructor challenges students to consider the nature of several key assumptions underlying the education process (K–college) in the context of their own personal experiences with schooling. This process, depending on the level/age of the students, can take anywhere from five minutes to five days. The key is to get students to appreciate their own experiences as paramount in the interpretation of their educational goals and behaviors, as opposed to conjured narratives about the function/purpose/benefits of school. Next, the instructor outlines their ideas about challenges in traditional education and invites students to connect their own experiences with the descriptions of the educational experiences. The instructor concludes by explaining that the current course was designed to intentionally confront the oppressive tendencies of the banking system of education by requiring students to think critically about the course material, themselves, and their own unique interactions with the ideas to be discussed. The instructor then thoroughly and carefully describes the concept of structured dialogue (which is detailed further in Stage 3) and asks for input about how the process should proceed, attempting at every opportunity to incorporate students' ideas and suggestions into classroom norms and rules.

Stage 2: The instructor orients students to material (textbook chapters, course readings, videos, etc). This is done in a cursory fashion where the instructor is careful to point out that the presentation is fully intended to be their interpretation of the material. Personal stories, interpretive anecdotes, and direct and rhetorical questions are emphasized during the presentation in order to maximize student involvement and elaboration. Wherever possible, the instructor should highlight original or controversial ideas, as well as speculations and skepticisms, in order to clarify the tenuous, uncertain nature of the information presented. At the end of the presentation, the instructor invites students to offer their ideas (generated by the presentation and/or course material) for structured dialogues.

Stage 3: A structured dialogue exists when an individual presents an idea to the class for the purposes of obtaining their collective critiques and thoughts on it. The obtaining process is twofold. First, the individual writes the idea on a chalkboard or whiteboard for all to clearly and plainly see, at which point the class is given the opportunity to ask questions for clarification (all questions must be strictly clarifying in nature, and are not meant to challenge or interrogate the implications, antecedents, or significance of the idea on the board). After all questions for clarification have been sufficiently addressed, individuals are allowed to present their objections to the idea. These objections are called "counters" because they counter the idea as presented. Counters must be presented one at a time. After each counter, the idea originator has the opportunity to engage the counter originator in dialogue about the counter. During the dialogue, the remaining class members are not to interrupt or participate in the dialogue with comments, gestures, or questions. After the counter is clarified and addressed by the idea originator, a new counter (by the same individual or by another) can be made. This process continues until all counters have been communicated. At this point, a vote is held as to who in the class agrees with and endorses the idea as presented on the board.

Stage 4: During the structured dialogue, the instructor takes note of key aspects of the idea originator's stance. The most important prerequisite for quality structured dialogue is preparation. It should be evident that any counters presented were anticipated by the idea originator; only the idea originator is graded. Concision is also extremely important, as is the ability to produce examples and illustrations to support the idea and directly address counters from others. Comments are invited from those who observed the dialogue(s). Comments can be topical, but should ideally focus on the exchange(s) witnessed.

The African Cultural Basis of SDM

The SDM is situated within several ancient African and contemporary African American cultural traditions of oral communication. The SDM is consistent with the tradition of an open, secret society for Africans to learn the skill sets of secrecy and verbal parry. Indeed, embodied within the African intergenerational communication arsenal are a number of different proverbs, riddles, and word problems (Jackson-Lowman, 1997) that may be applied to a given dilemma or response pattern to solve problems or elevate communal understanding and intelligence. Several African oral traditions may be included: *Sarbeeb*, a form of oblique communication from Somalia (Samatar, 1997); proverbs, which provide a system of logical, metaphorical, and symbolic relationships between entities; and riddles from the Shona (the native language). Moreover, within the African tradition in Ghana, the Adinkra symbol *mate matsie* translates to, "I have kept what I have seen." These models seen within the traditional societies of Africa pre-date colonialism. SDM resembles an *mbongi*. The *mbongi* is a Kikongo institution that creates a critical political meeting space for discussion among community members on issues central to the well-being of the community (Fu-Kiau, 2007).

The SDM is also closely tied to the sociopolitical context of being African in America. Jedi Shemsu Jehewty's concept of the "intellectual maroon" (Black thinkers who have "declared their freedom" from European intellectual bondage) represents just such a reconstruction. In a seminal article titled "Intellectual Maroons: Architects of African Sovereignty," Hotep (2008) formally identified three major "landmarks" on the road to intellectual maroonage:

1. Intellectual disobedience
2. *Nyansa nnsa da* (a Twi term meaning, "wisdom has no limits.")
3. Liberational logic

The SDM encompasses and facilitates each of these, which are discussed individually below.

Intellectual Disobedience

Intellectual disobedience refers to the intentional breaking of the rules (written and unwritten) that guide and fortify academic disciplines and the structure of higher education itself. When one considers the fact that the Euro-domination of ideas and knowledge has resulted in what has been classically termed the "miseducation of the negro" (Woodson, 1933), intellectual disobedience becomes nothing short of a prerequisite for intellectual decolonization. Examples abound. Consider the study of history, as Kambon (2012) discussed in *African/Black psychology in the American context* (62).

> Eurasians have colonized world knowledge about Africa (i.e., Africans and their beginning and development through time) in an effort to enforce White/Eurasian supremacy domination over the world (over Africans to be precise). This strategy has consequently distorted/disguised and misinterpreted/misrepresented ancient African knowledge, civilization and historic events, taking them out of their natural cultural context and falsely projecting them as Eurasian-centered in nature. This allowed the Europeans/Eurasians to literally write (at least attempt to write) Africans completely out of substantive world history. In this effort, for example, they have through fabrication and distortion credited the Greeks and other Eurasians with the creation of what was actually African knowledge and civilizations (Ani, 1994; Ben-Jochannon, 1982; Clarke, 1991; James, 1976, J. Jackson, 1980).

The example of history begets a broader issue of the reality of European cultural domination of world knowledge (Ani, 1994).

Among the most compelling aspects of the SDM is its tendency to encourage individuals to disagree with, resist, and ultimately reject standards of European intellectual authority. Although educational curricula are dictated by a power structure oppositional to African communities, and political and social interests, discussions with the SDM tend to center on the implications of that curricular power structure for African people. This is due (in part) to the fact that dialogue requires authentic thought and human connection. Eventually, the system's conventions themselves become exposed for what they are: arbitrary rules intended to suppress African thought resistance (Ball, 2011) to cultural invasion.

Nyansa nnsa da

Nyansa nnsa da is a Twi term meaning, "wisdom has no limits." Hotep (2008) credited Garvey and Addae (1995) with the *nyansa nnsa da* paradigm, which holds that "African intellectual freedom, and by extension political and economic sovereignty, hinges on developing both the will and the skill to think and act outside of and independent from established Western categories and frameworks" (p. 8). Laila Afrika (2000) made this point in the foreword to his book *Nutricide: The Nutritional Destruction of the Black Race*:

> It has always irritated me to use Caucasian references when I write, it is as if an African cannot have an idea unless a Caucasian had it first. This Caucasian information control creates a "Scientific Plantation" and "Information Colonialism." (Afrika, 2000, p. xi)

Afrika's notion of information colonialism echoed Noble's (1986) assertion that "scientific colonialism" distorts the African origins of information and ideas, allowing political entities to intellectually usurp them in an effort to appear intellectually superior. Hotep went on to write, "At its highest expression, *nyansa nnsa da* brings forth models of excellence rooted [in] our highest African cultural values and philosophical principles. ... Among other skills, mastering the art of shifting seamlessly from 21st century Caucasian to ancient or traditional African modes of thought and feeling is paramount for Africans in the Diaspora" (p. 8). The SDM embodies *nyansa nnsa da* by honing a particular skillset that involves bringing "one's own true energy/spirit" to bear on the proceedings.

Another facet that situates the SDM in the African tradition is its participatory nature where participation is required, and spectatorship is not acceptable. There is no audience, only community. The SDM is not for spectators; it is a spiritual, community activity that thrives off of growth. The individual grows intellectually by having their thoughts challenged in new and unpredictable ways. The community grows by accumulating meaningful ideas relevant for its liberation and sovereignty. There is not one way to engage; and each thinker-fighter, and thus each dialogue, is different. In addition to the course material, students *learn* to bring forth their own style of intellect and creativity. Thus, as an African-centered exercise, Structured Dialogue necessarily involves the spirit realm. According to Richards (Ani, 1980), "Enlightenment, and the acquisition of wisdom and knowledge depend to a significant degree on being able to apprehend spirit in matter."

A second critical aspect of the *SDM* is that it successfully shifts the origin of the idea/dialogue from the power stakeholder (e.g., professor) to the oppressed/marginalized, who are typically unashamed of their particular motive or agenda. Dialogues are not seen as academic, neutral, sanitized debates about facts; rather, they are seen as intense and often emotional displays of wisdom, vulnerability, and spirit-filled community. Recall that each dialogue is personally meaningful to the idea presenter, and by extension, the community. Thus, when an individual presents their idea, they are literally hoping to fight for it in the best interests of community. This is exactly opposite to the traditional model of academic achievement, which rewards and celebrates "learning" by singling out an individual for honors, awards, grades, degrees and the like. Each dialogue, whether won or lost, intellectually benefits African communities.

Liberational Logic

Hotep (2008) also detailed Maulana Karenga's (1997) concept of "liberational logic," as a landmark on the path to intellectual maroonship, which is defined as "reasoning directed toward undermining and overthrowing constraints on human thought and practice" by "promoting conscious emancipatory activity on the intellectual and practical level" (p. 9). In *My Ishmael*, novelist Daniel Quinn uncovered the essence of the latent structuring of education:

> What one sees first is how far short real schooling falls from the ideal of "young minds being awakened." Teachers for the most part would be delighted to awaken young minds, but the system within which they must fundamentally frustrates that desire by insisting that all minds must be opened in the same order, using the same tools, and at the same pace, on a certain schedule. The teacher is charged with getting the class as a whole to a certain predetermined point in the curriculum by a certain predetermined time, and the individuals that make up the class soon learn how to help the teacher with this task. This is, in a sense, the first thing they must learn. Some learn it quickly and easily and others learn it slowly and painfully, but all eventually learn it. (p. 131)

Freire's (1970) critique of what he referred to as the banking system of education in *Pedagogy of the Oppressed* has tremendous relevance. In the banking model of education, knowledge and information are viewed as being given by teachers (who are assumed to be wise and knowledgeable) to students (who are considered ignorant). This situation results in a fundamentally contradictory and oppressive relationship, which "negates education and knowledge as processes of inquiry" (p. 72). According to Freire, banking education maintains and even stimulates the inherent contradiction that exists between the student and the teacher, which ultimately never allows the student to realize that they can (and in our experience, often do) educate the teacher. The SDM epitomizes the liberational logic paradigm in that it extends the dialogue around critical issues, research, and perspectives for African people on a regular, recurring basis. As will be seen, the instructor plays a very different role in the SDM compared to traditional/Western pedagogical modes.

Finally, the SDM has considerable potential for reducing the harmful, deleterious effect of White supremacy on Black college students. By candidly exposing the constricting nature of curricula and the oppressive tendencies of faculty, the SDM allows students to engage instructors not as authority figures who dole out meaningless (if not psychologically harmful) information and marginalize their perspectives, but as helpful, healthful mentors who nurture their development and allow their own particular talents and genius to flourish. The SDM then, serves as a training model for the developing African intellectual mind. Fostering a free space for students to deliberate about what they are genuinely interested in, while simultaneously requiring them to expose their thought process for the community forces the serious student to think deeply about their position. Most often, this has the effect of moving students toward those ideas that are marginalized and omitted from traditional mainstream discourse and curricula. Such ideas make plain the nature (what Ani [1994] has referred to as the *Asili* or "seed") of the culture that students find themselves in. It is this seed that higher education attempts to obfuscate. For example, higher education serves to politically indoctrinate and confuse African people about power relationships that have tremendous import for their individual, family and community lives. Such oppositional indoctrination is made possible largely by the reality that the political nature and implication of European ideology is denied and hidden by the educational institution.

Recommendation #3

Be sure to have someone knowledgeable about cultural studies and African/Black psychology involved in the planning, research procedures, analysis, and dissemination of community-engaged studies. The insights and patterns that they will offer will resonate with participants and enable recognition and credibility to the research team that will prove invaluable.

The Role of Black Psychology in Education

Many of the theoretical frameworks from the field of African/Black psychology center the discourse on the documented cultural worldview of African peoples (Ani, 1994; Baldwin, 1995; Kambon, 2012, Nobles, 1976; Hilliard, 1972). Many African scholars have argued that the distinct cultural and socioenvironmental conditions of Africans and Europeans reflect distinct racial-cultural histories and fundamental differences in their basic natures (Ani, 1994, 1997; Baldwin, 1980b, 1985; Carruthers, 1973, 1981; Diop, 1978, 1991; Nobles, 1976b, 1986b; Welsing, 1991; Wright, 1974). European American culture does not recognize the true cultural differences between itself and Africans in America; rather, it promotes such categories as "superordinate" and "subordinate," or "superior/advanced" and "inferior/primitive" when it comes to levels of a "universal," monolithic European culture (Kambon, 2012, p. 274).

Within the field of African/Black psychology, calls for culturally responsive pedagogy date back to the early 1970s. Hilliard (1972) demonstrated key differences in learning styles between African American and White children, and called for teacher training programs to equip educators with culturally based pedagogical tools to engage, motivate, and succeed with African American youths in the classroom. In a 1992 paper in the *Journal of Negro Education,* he recounted his efforts (dating back to 1976) to educate the California State Department of Education on the issue and existence of distinct cultural learning styles derived from the clear cultural differences between Africans and Europeans, particularly in language, religion, and music; a subsequent controversy erupted in the New York State Department of Education in 1992 over essentially the same issue (Hilliard, 1992). He stressed the "utility of behavioral style for instructional planning [as] dependent upon systematic study of the nature and potential of that style for teaching and learning" (Hilliard, 1992).

Recommendation #4

Encourage community leadership to disagree with each other and with members of their community. The ability to use disagreements to find opportunities for growth is very important, and can foster solidarity, trust, and conviction—valuable characteristics of any group facing high-stakes challenges. In many ways, the dialogic process is intimate. It requires trust and sincerity and thrives on intentionality. As researchers, unless we see, respect, and understand how leadership arises and happens in local communities, we will not be able to leverage (as allies) those community leaders whose experiences, backgrounds, and organizational bases are outside of traditional fellowship/academic/policy circles. Disagreement is bound to arise throughout the process of community-engaged research.

Our goals in community-engaged research should be to understand what it means to invest in leadership that affirms and honors the lived experiences of people in communities grappling with systems of inequity. This requires reflective and potentially uncomfortable challenges to ourselves to not just think, but also move differently in order to avoid re-entrenching structural elements that contribute to Black and Brown death and disease. As we know, many communities have been historically violated by individuals, organizations, and institutions posing as "saviors." It is critical that we all value and partner with organizations that are sensitive to these realities, so we can hold each other accountable and behave in ways that acknowledge their power and potential for liberation.

Lessons Learned

To study Black and Brown communities in search of resilience is a problematic pattern guaranteed to ensure that cycles of poverty, miseducation, disease, violence, and death persist. This chapter calls instead for a dialogic model that brings individuals together with hopes that honesty and conviction will point toward solutions generated and exercised by those communities disenfranchised by generations of research and science. The recommendations offered in this chapter—speak openly about researchers' roles, encourage research participants to interact without the researchers, collaborate with someone knowledgeable about cultural studies and African/Black psychology, and encourage community leadership to disagree—should be seen as a tentative blueprint for building truly meaningful, engaged models that transcend "collaboration" and encourage honesty about Eurocentrism, White supremacy, and the importance of culture in the individual, family, and community lives of African people.

References

Afrika, L. O. (2000). *Nutricide: The nutritional destruction of the Black race*. A & B Publishers Group.

Ani, M. (1994). *Yurugu: An African-centered critique of European cultural thought and behavior*. Africa World Press.

Baldwin, J. (1965). The American dream and the American negro. *The New York Times*, 7, 32–33.

Ball, J. (2011). I mix what I like!: In defense and appreciation of the rap music mixtape as "dissident" and "national" communication." *International Journal of Communication*, 5, 278–297.

Boyd, D. (2008). A university serving the oppressed: A liberatory teaching paradigm for the college student of the future. *International Journal of Multicultural Education*, 10(2), 1–14.

Brown, B. (2006). Shame resilience theory: A grounded theory study on women and shame. *Families in Society*, 87(1), 43–52.

Burkhart, R. E. & Limaye, M. R. (2002). Attitudinal change and critical pedagogy: An exercise in a political science and global business course. *Journal of Teaching in International Business*, 14(1), 65–81.

Carruthers, J. H. (1999). *Intellectual warfare*. Third World Press.

Chilisa, B. (2019). *Indigenous research methodologies*. Sage Publications.

Curry, T. (2016). Eschatological dilemmas: The problem of studying the Black male only as the deaths that result from anti-Black racism. *I Am Because We Are*, 479–499.

Darwin, C. (1909). *The origin of species*. PF Collier & Son.

Freire, P. (1970). *Pedagogy of the oppressed*. Continuum.

Hilliard, A. G. (1992). Behavioral style, culture, and teaching and learning. *The Journal of Negro Education*, 61(3), 370–377.

Hopkins, K., Meyer, M., Shera, W., & Peters, S. C. (2014). Leadership challenges facing nonprofit human service organizations in a post-recession era. *Human Service Organizations: Management, Leadership & Governance*, *38*(5), 419–422.

Hord, F. L. & Lee, J. S. (2016). *I am because we are: Readings in Africana philosophy*. University of Massachusetts Press.

Hotep, U. (2008). Intellectual maroons: Architects of African sovereignty. *Journal of Pan African Studies*, *2*(5), 3–19.

Jackson-Lowman, H. (1997). Using Afrikan proverbs to provide an Afrikan-centered narrative for contemporary Afrikan-American parental values. In J. K. Adjaye & A. R. Andrews (Eds.), *Language, Rhythm, and Sound: Black Popular Cultures Into the Twenty-First Century* (pp. 74–89). University of Pittsburgh Press.

James, G. G. (1954). *Stolen Legacy: The Greeks were not the authors of Greek philosophy, but the people of North Africa, commonly called the Egyptians*. Philosophical Library.

Jernigan, M. M. & Daniel, J. H. (2011). Racial trauma in the lives of Black children and adolescents: Challenges and clinical implications. *Journal of Child & Adolescent Trauma*, *4*(2), 123–141.

Kambon, K. K. (2012). *African/Black psychology in the American context: An African-centered approach*. Nubian Nation Publications.

Karenga, M. (1997). *Kwanzaa: Origin, concepts, practice*. Kawaida.

Louis, K. S. (2006). Changing the culture of schools: Professional community, organizational learning, and trust. *Journal of School Leadership*, *16*(5), 477–489.

Masten, A. S. (2018). Resilience theory and research on children and families: Past, present, and promise. *Journal of Family Theory & Review*, *10*(1), 12–31.

Nobles, W. W. (1986). *African psychology: Toward its reclamation, reascension & revitalization*. Institute for the Advanced Study of Black Family Life and Culture.

Parker, P. S. (2004). *Race, gender, and leadership: Re-envisioning organizational leadership from the perspectives of African American women executives*. Psychology Press.

Rhoden, W. C. (2010). *Forty million dollar slaves: The rise, fall, and redemption of the Black athlete*. Broadway Books.

Shumway, D. R. (1989). Reading rock'n'roll in the classroom: A critical pedagogy. In H. A. Giroux & P. McLearen (Eds.), *Critical Pedagogy, the State and Cultural Struggle* (pp. 222–235). State University of New York Press.

Sleeter, C. E. (1996). *Multicultural education as social activism*. State University of New York Press.

Smith, L. T. (2013). *Decolonizing methodologies: Research and indigenous peoples*. Zed Books.

Vella, J. K. (2008). *On teaching and learning: Putting the principles and practices of dialogue education into action*. Jossey-Bass.

Williams, R. L. (1974). The death of White research in the Black community. *Journal of Non-White Concerns in Personnel and Guidance*, 2(3), 116–132.

Wilson, A. N. (1993). *The falsification of Afrikan consciousness: Eurocentric history, psychiatry, and the politics of white supremacy*. Afrikan World InfoSystems.

Chapter 6

The Gift of Resilience Among Youths from Oakland

Regina Jackson

This chapter pulls from my experiences as the President and Executive Director of the East Oakland Youth Development Center and as a community partner engaged in research. I provide a reflection on how we decided to engage in research and how trust and honesty were critical components in building the research relationship. I discuss the deep sense of responsibility I felt in protecting the youths we serve, while also weighing the research benefits to the larger community. My engagement across several research projects—including one funded by the Robert Wood Johnson Foundation—led me to see the unique ways community-engaged research can and does create opportunities for youth and communities to build resilience and strength.

Since I was a little girl, I have loved stories of triumph—the stories where the characters focused on the response, and ultimate resolution to problems. Whether it was books or movies, I was invariably interested in new worlds with new problems to tackle. No doubt this captivation has had a tremendous influence on my role in the world. The main difference, though, is that this is the real world—and in the real world, problems are not so easily responded to or resolved. I believe that non-profit organizations are one of the most effective real-life transformers of communities. They are a true counterweight that, when introduced efficiently, eases the pressures of a volatile environment and its effect on the generations that inhabit it for both those living there by choice and those confined by circumstance.

My whole world turned on its axis in 2008 at a meeting to introduce the East Oakland Building Healthy Communities initiative (EOHBC, 2021). Established by the California Endowment, this 10-year, $100 million dollar undertaking was designed to identify community-engaged research and public health opportunities within extremely underserved communities. The Endowment identified ten communities throughout the state of California, with East Oakland among them. East Oakland is a microcosm of challenges that manifest across health, education, economics, and violence. In urban spaces with highly disenfranchised communities, there is a preponderance of joblessness, health inequities, gang violence, drug use, and desperate behavior. This initiative was the start of a mental shift, both in my field and in my community. This approach was a change in our fundamental thinking on the subject overall.

One hundred percent of the East Oakland Building Healthy Communities partners hailed from our community. Stakeholders were part of an elaborate strategy to utilize our various areas of expertise to design and implement action plans and programs to obviate the health issues that harmed our communities most. A host of individuals and organizations who focused on health and wellbeing attended these meetings. Some I knew well and were top in their field; others I only knew by name. Seeing the wide range of experts joined together for one common mission, I thought to myself, "These are excellent partners with proof positive legacies. We are totally capable of responding to this challenge!"

Along with hope for the future, the initial intrigue of this initiative was the promise of funding for our organizations. But what once was intrigue had become inspiration. The opportunities that lay ahead were like magic in the making. I experienced an immersion of sorts, where I was learning a new language and tactics, and received the kind of development tools that our nonprofit could never have afforded. I heard words like *texturize, traction, methodologies, frameworks, contextualization*, and *logic models*—terms I was familiar with, but more in relation to my hairstylist than my work. This speaks to the great divide that is our society—there are people speaking entirely different languages and dialects. So many organizations on the front lines are pushing so hard to do the work, they rarely have the mechanics to promote, advance, and excel. My head was swirling as if I was experiencing an information-overload-induced brain freeze. I took a second to efficiently process this new wealth of information. It was a new language, so I learned the language. I understood that it was a crucial part of academic and philanthropic linguistics. We nonprofits were invited to design the master plans, using our frontline knowledge like military architects to inform a coordinated approach to improvement in our neighborhoods. We had secured a place at the table and were sitting "in the room where it happens" (á la Hamilton) with action plans, think tanks, and blueprints as the tools for empowering our community.

Over the course of several months, we learned about the initial research conducted in the various sectors in East Oakland. We discussed next steps and began to work together to identify our special connections to the work and frame our 10-point plan of attack for the public health challenges in our own backyard.

This singular experience helped a lot of our organizations make a critical transition in how we approached our work. Some were already very data-savvy, while others were just getting data-curious (I was among those others). The Endowment later funded our organization to conduct youth-fueled research to identify mapping gaps and design logic models and strategic plans, which would inform our work and how we reported on it. Measurable outcomes, objectives, and tactics helped our organization pivot to compete in a new world of next-generation nonprofits where research was informing and evolving the actions we took. We had acquired an expansive toolkit to prove influence. Our organization was finally positioned to move into new realms and deepen its work and impact.

LeConte Dill

Then she walked in. Enter LeConte Dill, a Doctor of Public Health (DrPH) candidate at UC Berkeley; she was a woman with an infectious smile, warm spirit, undeniable passion, and an underlying Black Panthers approach to advocacy. Originally from South Central LA, her powerful identity had been deepened by a historically Black colleges and universities (HBCU) education received at none other than Spelman College.

Sent at the recommendation of the California Endowment's program officer, Sandra Davis, Dill was proposing for her doctoral dissertation the interdisciplinary community-engaged research project we didn't know we were waiting for. She described the project enthusiastically, and as she spoke I could visualize the Star Trek experience we were about to embark on: "going where no man's ever gone before." Her aim was to have young people document their routes to resilience in our war-torn killer corridor of deep East Oakland, my stomping grounds. The East

Oakland Youth Development Center (EOYDC) is a central location in this urban warzone, where the area's highest rate of homicide[1] surrounded us in all directions. EOYDC provided a beacon of hope; it was like an oasis in the desert providing both leadership skills and training and love and hope to all who visited, particularly those in the immediate surrounding neighborhood.

Dill hoped to angle her research through storytelling, using poetic language to teach the process of community-engaged and participatory action qualitative research. Excited about the possibilities for both the research and experiential learning for our youth, I said yes! As a community leader, I'm an old-fashioned risk taker and recognize value in doing new things and shaping new experiences. Instinct comes with the experience and territory. Fortunately, moving on whispers is often how nonprofits access opportunities, form partnerships, and address issues. Unconstrained by fear or defensiveness, I was told that many executive directors would not be so brave or trusting to allow a complete stranger into our world for the purpose of digging deep into our children's lives for research. I was open to learning and open to research, recognizing that the data collected might be expansive; for our own data-curious minds, this could prove helpful to the organization and our funders. But the most extraordinary opportunity lay in what it would do for our children. To pivot and treat them as subject matter experts of their own experience would build upon the general value and respect for the youth voice that we already had. Further, the shared experience of telling their stories could empower and affirm them beyond the moment and document this special journey in ways we never had before.

---

1. Over 33% of homicide victims in Oakland are between the ages of 15 and 24 years (Beyers, Jain, & Mena, 2006), and 61% of the homicides in Oakland occur in East Oakland (Spiker, Garvey, Arnold, & Williams, 2009).

I vetted Dill through phone calls and emails, and the results confirmed my gut feeling that she was the real deal. While most of the research world had one identity—dominated by older, White male voices—she was none of these qualities. Her identity was empowering. The goals and aspirations she had for the process promised new emerging strategies for pushing boundaries in community-engaged research. Proposing a combination of community identity and academic research, Dill realized the tremendous responsibility of accessing youth experiences in order to facilitate understanding, both inside and outside of the organization. She also understood the ongoing value of documentation, not only through her dissertation, but also through conference participation and academic journals—none of which EOYDC had been involved with in the public health space. We were creating a whole new depth to how we show our receipts. Our receipts are our version of proof, examples, and experiences that demonstrate what happens in real-world scenarios.

We have always valued the power of youth voice, and now we were going to exponentially amplify it. We recognized that our community is capable of understanding theories and taking those theories to action, all with our youths at the forefront.

The first method was also the most important: allowing the researcher to know the community. This concept harkens back to a quote I use all the time: "Start out the way you want to end up." We invited Dill to conduct her data collection through observant participation, and encouraged her to come sit in our bird's nest. Imagine all she could learn by watching double Dutch—identifying the different responsibilities of the rope turners and jumpers and digesting all the sideline commentary. She observed many different programs in several different spaces, all within the comforts of our campus. We invited her to events both on-and offsite. This allowed the outsider to become an insider, a familiar face.

All of this reminded me of a field trip where we visited author and Black Panther, Angela Davis. Dill commented on the care we showed our youths, encouraging their participation by asking questions and later by taking each child home one by one. It all screamed *family*—that second home the students refer to when they talk about EOYDC.

After some time of observation, Dill noted that EOYDC's approach was different from that of other organizations. Others tended to assign clear and decisive roles from the onset; who is the academician, the researcher, the data analyst? She witnessed how restrictive this process was and how it then precluded everyone from comprehending the definition of community. EOYDC was different. We had to be flexible and allow the experience to take shape as we developed, not wanting to miss any of the gifts that unrestricted participation provided.

The Project

Dill wanted to focus on approximately 20 older adolescents (i.e., high schoolers) for the study, but given that youths of different ages also face the same risks and experiences, I encouraged the additional inclusion of five middle schoolers. While a younger voice might not be as skilled in communicating, we knew that their voices were not typically given center stage. What might we miss by excluding them? As we discussed it further, we realized the younger voices would prove to be the true gem of the project. These young voices provided the possibility for longitudinal data, as they could continue growing and sharing their experiences throughout the research process. Typically, when older students move on to college or work, they are replaced by students from the younger generation, creating a new cohort of students who can participate in the research. However, by expanding the age range of participants, the project could include access to both the OGs (alums, or members of the "older generation") and the BGs ("baby generation"), which had the potential to add important context to the youth development framework at EOYDC.

In addition, Dill wanted to introduce an art-based research component in the form of poetry, establishing a precedent. She was breaking down barriers with her cutting-edge approaches and our youths would benefit from it all. Setting the tone for this project required trust and acceptance for both this new venture and Dill herself. This was critical but was eased by the fact that the youths trusted me as their leader and that this was not the first time I'd introduced them to a stranger for the purpose of their development.

I began to prepare my 25 students, whose ages ranged from 12 to 20. I primed them for the process of meeting, sharing, and opening up to a stranger through poetry-informed research. We discussed the task of storytelling, which included poetry as a frame for documentation. Unsurprisingly, the youths were very curious and even excited at the prospect. We were unsure of what the outcomes would be and unsure of the project's full timeline, but I could sense the masterpieces and hidden perspectives unlocked through the power of unrestricted freedom of expression. We were committed to flowing with it and checking in session after session.

The First Session

During our first meeting, welcomes and introductions were made while setting expectations for engagement. We focused on the fact that the most valuable outcomes would come from openness, trust building, and curiosity in this new and unfamiliar space. Just outside the door, they could find comfort and encouragement from me if they had concerns or felt confusion. That said, as a more familiar face inside the center, the deck was stacked in Dill's favor, and her experience and transparency led the way. The richest and deepest results would come from their collective uninterrupted engagement and would be uniquely theirs to design and disseminate.

At the end of the first session, the youth leaders inquired of Dill, "You are coming back, right?" As the conversations continued, Dill did some member checking with me—an in-depth interview where she shared a recap of the session and tested theories. As we chatted in my office, I leaned back proudly, confirming and affirming, "Of course they said that." This was a very intentional member check with the Executive Director. Dill had come with her own theories and students were building on, confirming, affirming, and refuting *different* theories. It was important to share these theories with the organization leader to talk through personal struggles, privacy issues, and any concerns for personal safety.

Week after week, the taped individual and group sessions began to formulate themes of resilience. The participants looked forward to each session, as it created an outlet for them to tell their own stories and share life experiences—which also revealed vulnerabilities, affirmed empowered decision-making, and facilitated their gelling as a writing community. We were building a culture of health. Themes centered on spirituality, family, and safe spaces. While the group was diverse in ethnicity, age, and gender, everyone wore the EOYDC badge.

They all referenced themselves in the positive youth development framework the organization boasted. The concept of belonging was both important and undertheorized. The youths declared themselves "youth leaders"—responsible, hard-working individuals whose work was expected to be excellent. They all embodied this confident and serious identity, from the youngest to the eldest, and reinforced each other throughout each meeting. They were taught how to look at data and check for gaps and learned how to identify thematic analysis and unplanned interventions.

Similarly, member checking continued, which gave the Executive Director an opportunity to "be in the room" while still outside of the actual experience. The importance of positive reinforcement cannot be understated. Encouraging the students while they participated in other EOYDC programs reinforced their self-worth and how they perceived it in relation to our larger community.

The Results

What formed was "My Identity Is Community," a research collective where students learned how to interpret and discuss data, and where poetry frameworks were built. Safety and coping were key findings from this collective work. Discussions around safety within and outside of EOYDC was prominent. For example, the concept of *Safe Routes to School* emerged. In the midst of neighborhoods plagued by violence where walking for wellness is a precarious feat, the theme of violence prevention arose as we talked about how to avoid "trap houses" (or drug dens). Aware that violence could pop off at any time at these sites, youth leaders did their best to avoid them at all costs, especially to and from school. Thus, the students developed alternate routes home, as they shared through active discussions.

The concept of safe spaces like EOYDC was frequently mentioned as a focal point by the youths. EOYDC was identified as a place that parents trusted and where people were able to be counted on to have good intentions. EOYDC engagement pushed people to think about others, as much as oneself. This togetherness and trust were strengthened through the concept of "squad goals" where questions arose like: How do you nurture your squad? Who do you cry to? And who keeps you sane?

In addition to steps towards safety, students relied on personal coping inside and outside of EOYDC. Spirituality, in particular, was uncovered as a coping mechanism, as well as practices through one's faith. For example, youths who believed in a higher being discussed church attendance as a coping strategy.

Poetry was a key form of member checking where new and recurrent themes emerged in the poems that the youths produced. A particularly interesting concept was intersectionality, where youths were comparing and contrasting positive and challenging perspectives in their lives. Approaching different perspectives of a similar space offered dynamically different possibilities. For perspective, a youth created this poem entitled "I Live on a Block":

> I live on a block between two corners, I hear Gas Team, Otha Side PTeam Lady Gas Circle Boys
>
> I hear them fighting, I hear them fonking with other cliques I hear about who beat up who or who shot who I have a couple friends who are involved I am a friend because somewhere in this mess we found common grounds but this is only one corner
>
> I peak at the other corner
>
> I hear my father telling me that I can be anything I want to be I hear him telling me to get my grades up so I can get out of here I hear my 3.3 GPA I hear hard work and I hear success

Below is another poetic message that illustrates youth experience with safe spaces, providing a landscape of insights to gang activity in Oakland:

> My unsafe space is a gang A gang is hard with the color Red splattered all over it Red for anger Red for blood Red for family Red for fallen tears Red for fallen soldiers
>
> My unsafe place is a gang I stay away because my personality won't let me go I stay away because I have seen too many people that are gone now because of this place People I have sat in class with spoken and held conversations People that I have breathed the same air with My unsafe place is a gang I stay away from this place because my best friend has called me too many times crying telling me that another person is shot and gone, gone because they were at this unsafe place

Before long, there were 95 pages of poetry, which gave birth to the poetry anthology that we titled, *Y U Gotta Call It Ghetto?*

Reflection

These youth leaders turned researchers turned published authors and public speakers were transformed through a process that occurred more than a decade ago, yet they still reflect on that experience as a driver for their leadership and student engagement today. It is the ultimate confirmation of the resounding impact of our methods.

During a regular check-in with Ja'Keemah, a first-generation, rising senior at Sonoma State University, I asked her to reflect on her memory of working on *Y U Gotta Call It Ghetto?* She said:

> I was reminded of where I was in life at the moment and how hard my middle school years had been. In the midst of that I felt so much pride, I could not only see how strong I was then but could also acknowledge my growth over the past 10 years. It brought back instant memories of riding the bus to EOYDC after school with my friends, also co-researchers and co-authors of the book. I can still

visualize the walls full of artwork and the long tables full of poetry in one of the rooms we worked in. As I am now conducting my own research and on the journey to graduate school, I especially appreciate this experience. Dr. Dill's project gave me a real world example of just how powerful research can be and how lives can be changed when people ask the right questions and are diligent with solutions.

Ja'Keemah's reflections echo so many of the original group of student researchers. Throughout our journey, so many unintentional conversations emerged with Dill, which created the platform for presentations together at the annual meeting of the American Public Health Association (APHA). We presented three years in a row. In 2010, we presented a poster. For 2011, we presented a poster and presentation. The 2012 APHA roundtable at the Moscone Center in San Francisco was particularly phenomenal because its entire presentation was youth-focused. During our roundtable discussion, the students took center stage. EOYDC youth leaders did what they always do—they led. Despite being two years out from the research, they were poised, proud, and comfortable speaking about what they learned and experienced. Academics marveled at the stories the youths told about the community-engaged research process, poetry writing, and public speaking opportunities they were featured in.

So what did a scholar from outside the agency learn from collaborating with the EOYDC? Dill said:

> I learned how to engage with mutual vulnerability, in community-accountable scholarship. I learned how to listen to multiple voices and that in centering young people (in youth participatory action research), you don't erase their adult mentors and family members, and you don't erase yourself as a researcher, either. I learned that participatory research is not just a "Berkeley" thing

and does not have to be a "risk" for the academy, it is really the only way that I know how to be a scholar, and how I train my mentees to enter into partnership and scholarship. I learned that research can indeed include play, and that this play is in fact rigorous.

As the project wrapped up, the youths were in an environment of constant love and reinforcement. Their interaction with visitors over periods of time are impactful, but the children know that while they are not permanent, the environment is. They effectively grow with the changes because they know they have a base and support system that will be there after the visitors have left.

As we continued to work together, I was able to help the now-doctoral-trained Dill revise papers, share curiosities, and enthusiastically support the work. There were diverse dissemination channels for the research, which included university classroom presentations, APHA conferences, and four journal articles that were published. In one journal article, Dill referenced the "social capital"—a term that we actualized but did not use back then—created for our youth from our own work together (Dill & Ozer, 2019). The collaboration with Dill also ended up creating social capital for me, in the form of access to multiple professors at UC Berkeley Graduate School of Public Health.

Although our collaboration worked out beautifully, what kinds of challenges might this collaborative work present, and how can scholars be overcome from a methodological point of view? When presented with this question, Dill responded,

> This collaboration spoiled me into thinking that all partnerships would work so well. Me "hanging out in the bird's nest" of EOYDC for 6 months before I submitted an IRB application, and 9 months before I was granted IRB approval can serve as a model for entree with a community-engaged research project. Time to just be, to

hang out, get to know one another, before grants, protocols, and formalities. Also the member checking that I did at the end of the formal interview phase, including the poetry workshop to present preliminary findings with the youth, conversations with Ms. Regina in her office about my theoretical hunches, going on field trips with the group, that type of closure or adjournment should also be a model for other community engaged research projects. Also, it's important to remember that academia and non-profit organizations have different timelines, different ebbs and flows in their seasons, different cultures around what's urgent and what can simmer.

New Opportunity

In 2014, we received an additional opportunity when another graduate student at the UC Berkeley School of Public Health emailed me about a community-engaged research project on identity formation among boys and young men of color in East Oakland. Stephanie Fong introduced herself as a medical and master's student at UC Berkeley–UCSF Joint Medical Program who happened to be a fellow Bishop O'Dowd High School alum, native of a neighboring town, and former classmate of my eldest son, Noah. Before graduate school, she had worked at an East Oakland school down the street from EOYDC. Her students left an indelible impression on her—particularly, how several students with incredible potential had internalized pervasive, negative messages about who they were and who they could become. What is the process of identity development, she wondered, and how could the people, communities, and institutions caring for Black and Brown youths promote healthier identity development? Her foray into these questions revealed a dearth of perspectives through the eyes of young people themselves.

Would I be interested in partnering to ask these questions of young folks at EOYDC?

Intrigued but proud of and loyal to the untold, rich experiences of this often-overlooked population, I agreed to meet to discuss further. Before our meeting, I again vetted our researcher. I made calls to UC Berkeley professors, who now were more like close acquaintances after the last research experience. They confirmed my gut instinct. The fact that we attended the same high school and knew some of the same people was also affirming. Fong's educational background, emotional intelligence, and demonstrated ability to thrive in diverse, multicultural settings matched our sensitivity requirements to, once again, open our students to an important, yet vulnerable, set of storytelling experiences. Even more important was that what might be divulged during the research process could trigger memories of abuse, shame, and lack of worth. Concerned about this possibility, I decided it was important to quietly participate and support to facilitate the trust-building process, which is typically slow for young men. But I had great faith in the empowerment that this experience could provide to counteract any of the negatives that could arise. All in all, I saw the positives heavily outweigh the negatives in every aspect of this new research project.

At our first meeting, Fong explained that she was interested in using self-portrait photography, interviews, and group discussions to understand how young men of color described their identities; what influenced the way they saw themselves, both positively and negatively; and how their identities impacted their decision-making, mental health, and resiliency. She asked for my input, given my decades of experience in positive youth development, as well as the recent *Y U Gotta Call It Ghetto?* study.

Further, she wanted to know what I thought about her, an Asian American woman, leading research among Black and Latino young men. My response was curiosity: "What do you think about it?" She shared that it was an important subject to study, the research had not yet been done in Oakland or elsewhere, and she thought she could do it well. She could demonstrate to these young men that people from other races and genders care deeply about their health and humanity; to the academic and medical communities, she could underscore the power of solidarity. She was speaking my language.

Her approach seemed open and well-intentioned, but that would not be enough. I needed to take Fong through the paces because of the precious lives she would encounter and be responsible for. I mentioned that the trust-building process is very slow, particularly for Black and Brown young men. I encouraged her to volunteer at the center first to do observant participation and to become a more familiar face. If her desire to connect and build trust was authentic—as I imagined it was, based on our back-and-forth conversation—then I could make it work because it was also an important subject to me. The great thing about Oakland is that diversity works to everyone's advantage. You can be part of a larger community without being the same ethnicity or race if you spend time in diverse circles. Acceptance can be swift and abiding if the effort is genuine.

The challenge that faced us was time. We were in the midst of a capital campaign renovation and expansion, with many of our programs operating irregularly. Other than our gymnasium, we were sequestered inside three portables, with operations running from an external school campus during the summer. Despite the physical limitations of our operations, I wanted to move forward as I recognized the promise of the project and the potentially priceless data that would emerge. The results from this study could go a long way in supporting male achievement and also give us insights into the sometimes-reckless behavior that our organization witnessed.

Within a few months, we had finalized the research protocol together and garnered IRB approval. Fong had begun to volunteer with our GED program. "The Portrait Project," as her master's thesis was dubbed, was ready for launch. A group of 13 young men between the ages 18 and 24 were invited based upon their diversity, strength, and commitment to follow through. Ranging from GED graduates to college scholars to a professional artist, all of these proud men of color called Oakland home. They represented another great crew taking the helm of a freshly christened ship of knowledge on its maiden voyage. I felt a familiar jolt of excitement. There was something so powerful in this formal recognition that they themselves were the subject-matter-experts of their own experience.

In the Air

I thought it imperative once again to kick off the initial meeting, then decided to stay in the room to observe the introductory socialization process, certain that if conversations got off track, I could anticipate and redirect. A sensational first group meeting followed. Most of the contributors knew each other from the center's college prep programs. Those less familiar blended in based upon their cadence, willingness to learn, and enthusiasm to participate. Everyone was welcoming, and all the participants understood this was a unique opportunity to shine the light on themselves, their friends, and their community. There was even one man who engaged in the first research experience with Dill, which only sparked more curiosity and built his confidence to continue in the subject matter expert role. I hoped that his input would inform those quiet corners if confirmations got sticky and sensitive.

After their individual "selfie sessions" and interviews, the young men came together for a focus group to clarify and expound upon emerging themes. I listened as many described Oakland as their "beach"—their place of refuge. Oakland was their hope for a brighter future, their common identity. They recounted their stories of pain, torment, resilience, and redemption. Everything from being followed around in a clothing store to being refused service in a restaurant, each young man had several anecdotes they could recall at the drop of a hat. No story was the same, although there were many familiar themes. They were aligned in their struggles for survival, success, and self-worth. They described their frustration at how their superb command of the English language somehow suggested that they couldn't be from Oakland.

Overall, participants described the general atmosphere of this project, as well as individual and group conversations, as "therapeutic." The Portrait Project offered a rare opportunity to decompress and speak and think freely. These safe spaces are seldom available for our young people, especially boys and men. Our young men have a tendency to quietly withdraw when it comes to emotions, burying those feelings down deep. However, in this situation, faced with such a unique offering in a trusted space, they responded jubilantly. Strong and sensitive leadership from Fong was an important part of the equation.

Later, as presenters at the 2015 National APHA conference, the audience was transfixed on Fong and the student presenter as they shared the results. The verdict: despite identifying with stigmatized groups, participants were proud to be men, Black or Latino, and from Oakland. Nonetheless, dissonance between self-defined identities and others' presumed identification had significant effects on how the participants expressed their identities and moved about the world.

At the project's conclusion, the young scholars presented two culminating gallery shows. The first was held at the EOYDC. Scores of proud, young, local men and women of color were mesmerized as the participants shared their experiences from the research project. A second exhibit, during a reception sponsored by UCSF Benioff Children's Hospital in Oakland, demonstrated that these champions for youths were determined to ensure that professionals in their community understood their plight and the drastic effects it had on their health and community as a whole. One participant remarked to the crowd:

> I would like for you all to try to think about ways you can help more young men of color succeed and blossom out of Oakland despite all the hurdles we must go through to do so. And if you feel you can't help, and then at least think twice before you clutch your wallet or purse when you see a young man of color on BART [public transit]. Because despite how we may dress, talk, or look we are all powerful and resilient and all we ask is to be understood and genuinely cared about.

Another young man, who was initially hesitant to speak at the podium asked after the event, "When can we do that again?"

Throughout this research, as I got to know Fong better, watched her demonstrate deep commitment to the work, and listened to her multi-level advocacy plans, something hit me—we had all benefitted tremendously from this rich, cross-cultural and interracial collaboration. Unbeknownst to me, this experience was another Star Trek mission possible. Fong's vision created a euphoric sense of freedom for us all.

Now-Dr. Fong Gomez and I have continued to collaborate as cheerleaders and advocates for youths in Oakland and beyond. In our article published in the *Journal of Adolescent Research* (Fong-Gomez, 2020), we shared our findings and encouraged educators, pediatricians, mental health and social work providers, and public health professionals to take a culturally humble, holistic approach to recognizing the complex, diverse identities of boys and young men of color.

The Gift—Lessons Learned

Our enriched experiences with community-engaged research created unique opportunities for staff and students to recognize that youths' subject matter expertise could solve some of the challenges our community faces. Our kids are resilient. Resilience is a requirement for their survival in neighborhoods that they rely on day in and day out, given the circumstances of their environment. Rather than encourage or promote, it highlights what is already within them. The study is more for the expert than the subject, because the expert has the highest potential to make an impact. Rather than measuring the impact of the study on the children, we should be measuring the knowledge gained from the study by the expert because that knowledge can be implemented at some point, and that is where you will see the impact on the subject.

The multi-level benefits to our youths and our organization at large continue to inspire and inform our work. And the opportunities keep coming. Based upon the research we had been doing, I was asked to be the subject matter expert of my own experience in joining Kris Madsen and Phillip Graham as an Interdisciplinary Research Fellow through the Robert Wood Johnson Foundation. Madsen was asking me to work with the city of Oakland to improve their youth summer jobs program, and to explore how youth development organizations like EOYDC can help youths develop social capital. I looked back on my educational journey—from Dill's proposal to a published book, from students to experts, from Fong's Masters project to groundbreaking discovery of male identity formation. This work was worth doing. It was a no-brainer. Once again, I jumped at the opportunity: "Dr. Madsen, I accept the challenge." To other community providers and organizers, I recommend that you seize opportunities to collaborate in research. Building trust, vetting research partners, and negotiating community members' roles in research activities is essential. Not all researchers or projects may be a good fit but when an opportunity arises, consider the many ways the research may build both individual and community resilience.

References & Additional Resources

Beyers, M., Jain, S., Mena, M. (2006). *Violence in Oakland: A public health crisis, Alameda County violent death reporting system 2002–2004*. Alameda County Public Health Department.

Dill, L. J. (2015). Poetic justice: Engaging in participatory narrative analysis to find solace in the "Killer Corridor." *American Journal of Community Psychology*, 55(1), 128–135.

Dill, L. J. (2011). *Y U Gotta Call It Ghetto?* Urban Diligence Press.

Dill, L. J. & Ozer, E. J. (2019). "The hook-up": How youth-serving organizations facilitate network-based social capital for urban youth of color. *Journal of Community Psychology*, 47(7), 1614–1628.

EOHBC (2021). *East Oakland building healthy communities*. http://eobhc.net

Fong-Gomez, S. (2020). The portrait project: Content and process of identity development among young men of color in East Oakland. *Journal of Adolescent Research*, 35(30), 341– 367. https://doi.org/10.1177/0743558420908801

Furman, R. (2006). Poetic forms and structures. *Qualitative Health Research*, 16(4), 560–566.

Jackson, R. (2017). *Oakland is my beach*. Huffington Post. http://www.huffingtonpost.com/reginajackson/oakland-is- mybeach_b_9555042.html?ncid

Jackson, R. (2017). *Bent not broken*. Huffington Post. https://www.huffpost.com/entry/bent-not-broken_b_9621908

Ozer, E. J., Ritterman, M. L., & Wanis, M. G. (2010). Participatory action research (PAR) in middle school: Opportunities, constraints, and key processes. *American Journal of Community Psychology*, 46(1–2), 152–166.

Spiker, S., Garvey, J., Arnold, K., & Williams, J. (2009). *2008 homicide report: An analysis of homicides in Oakland from January through December.* Urban Strategies Council.

Chapter 7

Promoting Resilience Through Community-Engaged Research with a Community-Based Clinician

Rachel Jones

This work was conducted as part of the Robert Wood Johnson Foundation Interdisciplinary Research Leaders fellowship program grant to promote a culture of health by engaging in community-based research aimed to decrease youth violence and improve overall wellness.

This chapter explores the process of how a well-established community clinician partnered with researchers to conduct community-engaged research and promote youth and family resilience in her community, while simultaneously building individual and organizational resilience. To best illustrate my journey as the community research partner, the chapter will offer lessons learned through successes, setbacks, and self-care that became evident during a three-year research project.

Background

My connection with the community began 20 years prior to this research study. After living in and raising children in the community, obtaining a bachelor's degree in sociology and a master's degree in educational, school, and counseling psychology at the local university, and engaging in community activism and volunteerism, I had a vested interest in the health of my community. By the time the research opportunity I discuss in this chapter presented itself to focus on improving health and decreasing youth violence, I was in a leadership role providing trauma-sensitive mental health services to youth and families in a ten-county region with nine separate clinics and over 50 employees.

As a licensed professional counselor, I was steeped in strength-based therapeutic approaches to assist youths and families experiencing hardship, adversity, and trauma within the community. Typical interactions with youths and families involved things such as intensive, home-based mental health services, school interventions, and offering assistance to families during court proceedings and inpatient psychiatric hospitalizations. Services I provided included crisis screening and assessment, individual and group therapy, and on-call crisis rotations. The work exposed me to various forms of trauma involving self-harm, suicide, homicide, domestic violence, sex trafficking, bomb threats, and other significant safety concerns for children, families, and the broader community. The work also exposed me to the way individuals, families, and communities can heal after experiencing adversity.

Though well-established in community-based work, I was inexperienced in community-engaged research. The agency I was initially employed with had historically not engaged in research projects. This was partly because of funding restrictions and partly because of client confidentiality and associated risks. Therefore, opportunities to participate in research were not common, which made this grant more appealing.

Though my interest was high, and the focus of the research fit well with the population we served in the community, committing to a three-year research project required agency planning. Some considerations for the agency were grant requirements and structure, potential research questions, how to protect participants' private health information, and the capacity to give my time to the project. The only way this could be accomplished was if an assistant director position was created to restructure responsibilities and delegate tasks. Once the grant proposal was accepted, I was excited to finally test whether trauma informed interventions would help families understand the impact of trauma and learn resilience skills to improve their overall health and decrease youth violence.

Research Project

This three-year, community-based research project utilized an interdisciplinary approach, and the research teams consisted of two university-based researchers and one community partner. It also involved a combination of conducting a research study and learning the culture of health leadership skills, which were defined in the chapter introduction. There were distinct goals for each year. Requirements included distance-learning courses, three in-person conferences per year, and weekly webinars. A variety of topics were taught and reviewed like ethics and barriers to community-engaged research, team resilience, community involvement in research projects, communication of complex concepts in simple ways to stakeholders, dissemination of results, and examination of policy implications for sustainable change. The first year aimed to build team cohesion, identify the target audience, develop the research project, and obtain Institutional Review Board (IRB) approval. The second year focused on recruiting participants and conducting the research study. The third year was to disseminate findings and examine and propose policy implications.

Resilience

My professional training focused on resilience and healing, which are the essence of therapy. Over the years, my understanding of resilience evolved. It started with a simple definition that resilience is being able to bounce back from adversity and function as well or better than before the adversity began. Drawing on the work from the Center for the Developing Child at Harvard (2015), below are some of the core concepts of resilience:

1. It requires supportive relationships and opportunities for skill-building.
2. It is a dynamic interaction between interpersonal predispositions and external experiences.
3. Learning to cope with manageable threats to one's well-being builds resilience.
4. Some children respond in more extreme ways—both positively and negatively.
5. Resilience can be developed at any age, though younger is easier.

Throughout my career, promoting and building resilience with children and families involved reminding families of past successes, instilling hope, and planning for recovery. Helping children and families identify strengths—no matter how seemingly small or insignificant—and teaching positive thinking skills to replace cognitive distortions were also effective. Children become resilient when their caregiver is stable and supported. This is achieved by providing families with material resources, supporting stable parent-child relationships and relationships with trusted adults, teaching self-regulation skills, and minimizing the amount of toxic stress in the child's environment (Masten, 2014).

Resilience was especially needed for the most vulnerable members of the community, including children, people of color, single-parent households, and people with mental health concerns because of high levels of distress and a resource scarcity. Over time, I realized that resilience was necessary not just for youths and families to promote a culture of health, but also for myself as a mental healthcare professional, as well as my agency and the surrounding communities. Community work was fast paced, rapidly evolving, and layered with trauma exposure. But there was also unending hope for the future and evidence that professionals, organizations, and communities strengthen and heal.

The familiar concept of "from surviving to thriving" was presented through various professional experiences when the topic of resilience was introduced. Upon further examination, I came to understand the difference between resilience and thriving. Resilience was the ability to bounce back to a state of similar functioning before the adverse incident. Thriving, by contrast, was the ability to grow from the adversity and function better (Carver, 1998). My work involved both—helping individuals and families survive a traumatic event and regain a sense of normalcy. And later, once stable and resourced, they could develop the ability to thrive, grow, and even mentor others through similar lived experience. The same applied to organizational and community resilience as well.

Community-based mental health interventions also brought multiple opportunities to work directly and indirectly with interdisciplinary systems including healthcare, juvenile justice, emergency response, law enforcement, recreation services, housing, faith-based or religious groups, education, addictions and recovery, domestic violence, child welfare, and employment services. What resilience looked like in these settings varied. The Community Resilience Framework, developed by the International Consortium of Organizational Resilience, highlights five systems (healthy environment, responsible governance, quality of life, strong economy, and a prepared system) that contribute to community resilience. When these systems are weak, a community is vulnerable. But when these systems are strong, a community achieves capital.

Resilience work with these systems often began with providing basic education about mental health symptoms and traumatic stress response for both employees and the people they served in the community. Only when professionals and leaders understand how they are personally impacted are they in a position to effectively solve problems of organizational resilience. For years before embarking on the community-engaged research project, I provided education, outreach, and consultation to various organizations. As these organizations became more aware of the role trauma played within the workforce and operations, they could invest in preventing secondary traumatic stress exposure and increasing resilience. The focus was often on compassion fatigue and compassion satisfaction. The latter refers to the positive rewards derived from the work, which play a critical role in individual and organizational wellness (Stamm, 2002). This focus on organizational resilience helped me forge strong connections with key community stakeholders in our community-engaged research project.

To best illustrate my journey as the community partner, I am separating it into three phases per grant year. Each phase offered valuable lessons on successes, setbacks, and self-care. Success and setbacks come with the nature of research and community-based work. Self-care is critical to building resilience. Often, a provider's journey toward self-care can parallel the organization's journey toward resilience. This is especially true of those in leadership roles within an organization and in its surrounding communities. Mental toughness, agility, and the identification of meaning and purpose are essential to providing any community and public service. Additionally, making connections, accepting change as a natural part of life, looking for opportunities of self-discovery, keeping things in perspective, and maintaining a hopeful outlook were essential to having personal resilience and being able to promote it within others (Palmiter et al., 2012). Embedded throughout the three phases are themes of resilience for youth and families, for myself as a professional, and for the organization and community levels.

Year 1

The first year of the community-engaged research passed quickly because of the time commitment and intensity of required activities and reports. Dedicated time for the project was expected to be eight hours per week. The grant offered the rare opportunity to strengthen our research team and develop our research project prior to conducting the study and disseminating results.

Successes

To begin, connections with my research partners were strong. We shared a sense of synergy and common goals, despite never having worked together before. Though my research partners were familiar with one another's professional accomplishments and work habits, I was new to the group, and was pleasantly surprised to learn how much our work intersected and how well we got along as a team. That would prove to be useful later when problems arose with our research project. In general, we were gaining momentum as a team.

Reports and various distance-learning courses required from the grant funder, revisions of the research proposal, the Institutional Review Board application, and internal agency paperwork were intensive in the first year. Because of the large size of my agency, there were dynamics that could have potentially delayed review or approval of the research timeline. Some examples include a requirement of oversight and approval from colleagues who were not connected to the research project, competing priorities deemed more important than research, and the daily rigor of community-based work, which regularly competed for my time and attention. Given these realities within the agency, the fact that our research team completed the required paperwork by deadline was considered a significant success. It allowed our research study timeline to remain on track. This provided our research team a solid foundation to move forward with the development of our research project.

Starting the process of creating an assistant director position was a considerable step in the right direction and initially brought me great hope. This position would allow for appropriate time and resources to focus on the research project and provide more stability and support for the workforce. This was critical for my ability to fulfill the community partner expectations of the grant. A portion of the grant funds were applied to research team member time on the grant. My research partners had reduced course loads to work on this research grant. However, I did not have a reduced case load, nor were the funds applied to my salary. For that reason, I was eager for the assistant director position to come to fruition.

Additional successes during this year were the feelings of usefulness and connection to the community to improve health and decrease youth violence. Receiving valuable community feedback about adjusting the age range of the research participants was helpful to shape the research project in a way that would maximize effectiveness and meet families at an earlier point in their journeys. My professional connections and relationships with local schools and juvenile courts proved to be value-added while exploring options and deciding on a revised proposal. Because our research team adjusted the age range of the youth participants from middle schoolers to third through fifth grade students, we decided on an intentional focus on a trauma-informed intervention for both youths and parents/caregivers.

Setbacks

An immediate setback dealt with confusion and agency disagreement about how participants would use mental health services while still protecting private health information. As previously mentioned, it was not a common practice for my agency to participate in research projects because of the risks related to client confidentiality and accessing medical records. A considerable number of meetings to explain the project and explore internal options were held. It became apparent that additional training would be required, both for our agency and our research partners, were private health information to be exchanged.

Other problems were specific to the assistant director position. Misleading communication and lack of direction stalled progress in the creation of that critical role. As a result, there was some delay in ongoing development of the research project. Additionally, my expected eight hours of work on the project were done after hours and on weekends because I did not have relief from regular job duties, despite earlier conversations about how the work on the research project could be completed during my typical work week. After sharing these concerns with other community partners in my research cohort, I learned this was not unusual. Community partners routinely conducted research outside of a demanding schedule fraught with occupational hazards like secondary traumatic stress exposure, constantly changing funding streams, strict deadlines, pressure from the community, a general lack of control of what might happen in the community, and the responsibility to respond in a way that promotes healing and safety.

During this stage of our community-engaged research, much of my attention moved away from the research project and toward regular job duties and unanticipated tragedy. One community in my region averaged one suicide every two months for two years. The community was traumatized by adolescents and transitional-age youths dying by suicide. The scrutiny from the public and the media exacerbated the senses of hopelessness and grief of citizens in the community. Drawing on research about resilience and trauma-informed community work (Gurwitch et al., 2007; Porter, Martin, & Anda, 2016), I played a part in the larger movement for that community to implement a better system for screening and responding to suicidal youths and young adults. The community needed critical information to assist with referrals, identifying prevention strategies that would be effective for youths and young adults in the community, and partnerships between key mental health, juvenile court, youth homelessness, and education services.

In the spring that same year, one of my employees was brutally murdered. The months-long homicide investigation was unexpected. While grieving, I was also leading a team of people who were grieving. For several weeks, my attention and energy shifted to organizational healing and resilience until things became more stable and manageable. Again, this meant my focus on our community-engaged research project was not the priority at that time, even though the work was important.

In leadership roles, sometimes the unspoken expectations are for the leader to remain calm and composed. These expectations often disregard how the leader is impacted spiritually, emotionally, and psychologically by an event. My colleague's death introduced a new set of responsibilities for me, which involved restructuring teams, delegating job responsibilities, rehiring, and more frequent consultation. Again, resilience building was a necessity. What distinguishes organizations from being successful or profitable and from being resilient largely depends on behaviors that help prevent organizational breakdowns and respond to adversity in a timely manner. Behaviors like being integrated, adaptive, self-regulated, and robust help distinguish resilient organizations (ICOR, 2016). We began to collectively heal by engaging in trauma-informed debriefing, deciding as a group how we would celebrate her life, and creating time and space for grieving while upholding our responsibility to focus on our work to serve the community.

Self-Care

Due to the traumatic loss of my colleague, I restarted counseling with my long-term mental health provider, which I routinely did throughout my career during times of distress. It was a healthy way to emote, learn new skills, reframe my situations, and be reminded of my ability to cope and recover.

During one of the in-person research conferences, some colleagues had an honest discussion about having too many responsibilities and not enough time and energy to dedicate to critical research projects.

Afterward, one of my research partners gifted me the book, *Essentialism: The Disciplined Pursuit of Less*, by Greg McKeown (2014). This book changed my life. Essentialism is explained as making the wisest investment of your time and energy to operate at your highest point of contribution. It offered a solution to what is termed "decision fatigue," which refers to having to make so many decisions that the quality of decisions deteriorate over time. I soon realized this would be an exercise in resilience.

By examining my professional goals and values, I noticed I was being pulled in several directions that were not in alignment with my training, purpose, or passion. Giving attention, focus, and my best energy to this research was a priority, but I had neither the time nor energy to devote. It was being wasted on tasks outside of my area of expertise and job scope. Without the assistant director as a possible solution, I had to get creative and courageous. Resilience sometimes requires radical acceptance, creative problem-solving, and the courage to assert one's needs. After reading the book twice, I began utilizing three new strategies:

1. I began using one notebook for everything—meetings, phone calls, task lists, etc.—which saved time and frustration from fumbling around and searching for where I put information. Meetings and consultations became more productive and focused because I could easily reference previous conversations and make clear decisions.
2. I wrote down the five most important projects I was working on at the time that were in alignment with my training, expertise, and purpose. This community-engaged research project was one of them.
3. I met with a supervisor and shared with her the five most important projects from my list; together, we outlined a plan to delegate

tasks to others. This allowed me to give other people opportunities to develop new skills of their own. It also held people accountable for doing their work. Additionally, this delegation freed up my mental creativity and energy to dedicate to what I was most passionate about.

Those three steps paved the road ahead over the next year to help me find balance and deeper sense of purpose in my work, and better utilize my knowledge and skills. It also fostered workforce development and provided other professionals an opportunity to step into important roles and share the burden of community mental health work.

As the first year closed, successes included being on track with required paperwork, courses, and a revised research proposal. Valuable community feedback helped us refine our research to include younger children to provide an earlier prevention for resilience building. The initial success of creating an assistant director position proved to be a setback as the position did not come to fruition. Though this put significant strain on my time and resources to focus on this important research, I took critical steps to establish professional boundaries. The most significant impact on my role as community partner in the first year was the trauma of suicide and homicide in my work outside of the research project. This sharpened my focus on personal, organizational, and community resilience.

Year 2

The second year was marked by a successful pilot, trouble recruiting participants, difficulties getting the research study started, and exposure to significant community trauma that pulled my attention and energy away from the research for a period. It was also a time when wellness became a priority and I made pivotal decisions to eliminate stress and forge ahead in a new direction.

Successes

Further development of our research study occurred in this phase. The study would involve a series of surveys and five sessions with parents to: 1) provide trauma education; 2) explain how trauma impacts child brain development; 3) explain how trauma impacts the parent–child relationship; 4) track how traumatic stress impacts physical health; and 5) explain protective factors and practice resiliency skills. We chose a previously developed curriculum, "Strong Parents, Stable Children" (Schramm et al., 2017). This curriculum involved five protective factors, which build child and family resilience: concrete support in times of need, parent resilience, knowledge of child development, supporting child social emotional competence, and social supports. Adding trauma and resilience education and promoting trauma-informed principles—safety, choice, trustworthiness, collaboration, empowerment—made for a more complete trauma-sensitive intervention to help decrease youth violence and improve overall health.

Recruitment flyers were sent to various places families and youth frequent, such as before-and after-school programs, grocery stores, laundromats, and faith-based organizations. Electronic flyers were also to be distributed through the school district's web-based platform. The initial pilot was a success and participant feedback was deemed valuable for next steps, which left us feeling encouraged that our intended impact could be achieved.

My continued focus on practicing essentialism carried over into this second year of the research project. Strategies continued to change and adjust with my job duties. It did not come without discomfort, awkward moments, and valuable lessons on letting go of control and removing my ego from projects I was deeply invested in. Resultantly, I began to carve out more appropriate time to dedicate to the community-engaged research goals and expectations. This was especially important because my role as the community partner included the responsibilities to finalize the intervention, train a research assistant to deliver the intervention, and oversee this component of the research study.

During this year, an unexpected job opportunity presented itself. Though it would take me away from providing services directly to the local community on a regular basis, it would expand my focus and influence on trauma-informed system change at a state level. In this new role, there would be broader, state-wide impacts across communities. I took the opportunity and began a new chapter in my career.

This decision had an impact on our research project because some of the components of the intervention relied heavily on the services my former agency provided. We made readjustments to the research project and did not lose the focus on building youth and family resilience. Fortunately, the child and parent surveys and parent interventions on trauma education and protective factors would remain. However, the changes we made to some components of the intervention did require us to resubmit to the Institutional Review Board and await approval. Ultimately, the research team saw this as a positive direction for the research project because it removed one of the biggest barriers to forward progress: the agency's concern for sharing private health information if a youth was to engage with mental health services.

Setbacks

Six gun-related homicides occurred within a two-week period in the community where we conducted community-engaged research. Victim ages ranged from 9 to 36, with the majority of victims adolescents and in their early 20s (Singleton, 2020). The deaths of youths and young adults was devastating. It only highlighted the need for our research intervention to be offered to as many residents as possible, since it aimed to decrease youth violence and improve health. By then, it felt even more imperative that we recruit research participants for the intervention.

Despite the sense of urgency, our recruitment efforts were largely unsuccessful for several weeks. The flyers that had been distributed to various locations were not yielding eligible referrals. Our primary recruitment base, the largest public school district in the county, had a cumbersome application process to post the recruitment flyer on their web-based portal. Initially, the district was excited about the research study, but the application process and multiple requests for information caused a delay that lasted an entire academic year. This was disappointing because it negatively impacted our research timeline. This experience highlighted systemic barriers that prevent people from accessing services, which then became another focus of the research project.

As with most setbacks, there is an opportunity to use a growth mindset instead of a fixed mindset, and to respond to challenges by changing how we think about our ability and talent (Dweck, 2008). After presenting information at one of our conferences, I felt frustrated and disappointed because we had anticipated being further along with our research study. One of my research partners and I decided to brainstorm and strategize. At this point, we felt strongly that our intervention would be helpful for youths and families. However, we encountered system-induced barriers, which made us question what other obstacles families experience when trying to participate in research studies or services.

While awaiting the district's approval we created an online survey to gather information about parent experiences with the schools and the mental health system. It helped identify trends in how schools responded to parents when their child had problems in the school setting, parent attitudes about their child being referred to mental health services, and other barriers that prevented families from accessing mental health services when offered. Another Institutional Review Board application was required and eventually approved. In addition to our pilot study, we now had a survey that provided valuable information regarding challenges families faced, like their own attitude about mental health services, schools recommending services but not assisting with accessing services, poor provider–client match, and inflexible provider hours and availability. We obtained over 1,000 parent responses to the survey from various states across the Midwest. This was a much broader reach than our research study, which was specific to just one county.

Self-Care

By this time, I was learning a new job and preparing for major transitions with my family, and I noticed stress-related physical health symptoms including migraine headaches, sleep disturbances, and tight, sore muscles that limited my range of motion. Not until I had this new job with a regular schedule, no on-call shifts, and more predictability did I understand the toll community-based mental health had taken on my brain and body. Things had improved a great deal, but there is always room to develop lifelong wellness habits that lead to greater resilience.

In my profession, I was accustomed to using the eight dimensions of wellness from the Substance Use and Mental Health Services

Administration and adapted from "A Wellness Approach" (Swarbrick, 2006). It highlighted eight domains that impact our functioning. The main idea is that these domains overlap and if they are not well-balanced, they begin to affect one another. It is all-encompassing and helps one focus on building skills and supports in areas of life that are sometimes overlooked, neglected, and even avoided. The interdependent domains are as follows:

> Emotional – Coping effectively with life and creating satisfying relationships.
>
> Environmental – Good health by occupying pleasant, stimulating environments that support wellbeing.
>
> Financial – Satisfaction with current and future financial situations.
>
> Intellectual – Recognizing creative abilities and finding ways to expand knowledge and skills.
>
> Occupational – Personal satisfaction and enrichment derived from one's work.
>
> Physical – Recognizing the need for physical activity, diet, sleep, and nutrition.
>
> Social – Developing a sense of connection and belonging and a well-developed support system.
>
> Spiritual – Expanding a sense of purpose and meaning in life.

Over the years, I used this wellness model in my work with clients, community partners, and employees. At this point, given my physical stress symptoms, I realized physical health practices like regular stretching, moderate exercise, decreasing my caffeine intake, and mindfulness could aid with focus and centering. Specific steps I took were to set up a small home gym and start low-impact body ball workouts, cardio dance videos, and Zumba classes. A consistent routine of deep breathing, meditation, and prayer, along with intentional quiet time in the morning before the rest of my family awoke, were critical to recovering from stress and adversity. The more resilient I became, the easier it was for me to notice a lack of resilience in others or in systems in which I was connected. Then I was able to provide education, resources, and strategies to assist organizations within the communities I served in becoming more resilient as well.

At the end of the second year, the study was better defined with trauma education and an identified curriculum. The pilot was successfully completed. Several recruitment flyers were distributed but the process for distributing them through the local school district was at a standstill. Emerging from that challenge was a new element of the research project: an online parent survey, which provided useful information about barriers to accessing mental health services that could later be shared with community stakeholders for process improvement strategies and to inform policy. Additionally, taking a new position required adjustments to the project and offered a new perspective into personal resilience.

Year 3

The third and final year of the research project gained momentum as we had about 20 participants engage in the small research study and we gathered preliminary findings. This year also brought about the unexpected global health pandemic, COVID-19. This impacted our research study and ushered in a new layer of adversity and opportunity to practice and promote resilience.

Successes

At the end of our three-year research project, four cohorts of participants had engaged in the community-engaged research. All but three participants were single parents and coordinating schedules proved to be problematic. In response, we transitioned the intervention to a web-based format. Questions arose about addressing family trauma and resilience through a telehealth approach. Ideally, face-to-face interventions would have been most beneficial to foster safe spaces and social connections. However, the web-based format was necessary to carry out the project, and it was successful. The participants responded well. It also removed barriers for participants including time, childcare, and transportation.

Our preliminary findings suggested parent trauma knowledge increased, parent stress and anxiety decreased, child distress decreased, and child efficacy increased. Parents and caregivers consistently voiced feelings of isolation, shame, and the belief that they were the only one going through problems with their child. They acknowledged that their own traumatic histories as children and adults impacted how they viewed their children and how they parented. Parents also reported they felt a sense of connection to other parents in the treatment intervention group and benefited from learning about protective factors and specific skills to use with their children. All participants were able to explain specific ways their child's behavior improved by using the resilience skills. One theme that stood out was that parental resilience was the protective factor they struggled with most. Sharing my own journey toward resilience was helpful in offering practical steps other parents could each take to achieve wellness.

One of the research assistants completed an interdisciplinary review of trauma-informed policies in the local school, juvenile court, mental health, and other youth-serving systems. Results uncovered a lack of policy specifically pertaining to the impact of trauma on youth and family health and violence prevention. This provided our research team the future opportunity to discuss why trauma and resilience should be included and how it could influence policy moving forward.

The skillset community-engaged research afforded me was beneficial for other opportunities in related areas, but those areas were outside of the research project. More specifically, those skills included how to share complex concepts in a palatable manner, using clear visualization to highlight key concepts, identifying key community stakeholders and including them in project development, using creative problem-solving to address barriers, and utilizing social networking to disseminate information and build upon existing resources. Opportunities that arose outside of the community-engaged research were being a keynote speaker at the Youth Violence Prevention Summit in the community that experienced the rash of gun-related homicides, writing articles on trauma-informed care in a national journal and magazine, and developing and hosting a webinar series to promote an organizational culture of resilience during the COVID-19 pandemic.

Setbacks

The two most notable challenges of this final phase of the research project were the delayed start and COVID-19. Based on the research timeline, by this stage in the project we should have been finishing the study and disseminating findings, including meeting with participants and community stakeholders to discuss implications of the work. Instead, the problems we encountered in the second year carried over to the beginning of the third year. This meant there was considerable angst about whether we would be able to conduct the study and have any findings to report.

COVID-19 impacted our research in three noticeable ways. Our momentum working together as a team abruptly changed. The recruitment from schools paused due to school closures, and our exit interview data were skewed because youths were no longer in a school setting where behavior could be observed. Since large group gatherings were canceled, our research team's annual conferences, the Youth Violence Prevention Summit, and regular research partner meetings were canceled. Due to the university closure, the research team conducted all meetings and participant interviews and surveys virtually. Since the intervention had previously transitioned into a virtual format, it was easier to conduct the study during the pandemic. But for a portion of the cohorts most impacted by the school closures, data about school behavior were missing. In response to the pandemic, the grant funder extended the time frames for research teams to complete projects, submit final research briefs, and expend funds related to the project.

Self-Care

The first part of the third year was manageable because I now had the time and resources to dedicate to the research. About halfway through the third year, COVID-19 impacted me in the sense that I was suddenly home-schooling my child and working a hybrid schedule. Job duties shifted to working with disaster recovery services for managing the pandemic. Once again, the focus temporarily moved away from the community-engaged research. Additionally, an unexpected and sudden death occurred in my family, which coincided with a required presentation with the research team and grant funder. Fortunately, my supportive research partners understood my circumstance and presented information in my absence.

The combined stressors caused me to be more deliberate about practicing and teaching resilience skills to our research study participants, employees, and citizens in surrounding communities. "Habit pairing" is the idea of pairing an old habit with a new one (Rubin, 2015). Because a habit is already established, doing a new activity during that time helps promote consistency and eventually develops a new habit. For example, saying positive affirmations while brushing teeth, meditation while drinking coffee, and working out while watching television can all promote resilience in everyday activities. I noticed in myself that these habits yielded positive self-talk, center and focus, pleasure, physical strength, stable moods, better concentration, restful sleep, and more creativity. These habits gave me a sense of clarity that allowed me to notice more quickly when I was off-balance and reacting from a stress response. The habit pairing concept was something I discussed with research participants in our study, as well as employees at my agency.

In response to COVID-19, I began leading employee wellness sessions and providing debriefings after COVID-related deaths. This was a unique opportunity to share resilience skills, coping strategies, and wellness education. In some cases, I was demonstrating the skills and guiding employees through activities like mindfulness, deep breathing, affirmations, applying a growth mindset, and replacing negative thoughts with positive ones. These sessions also focused on the concept of team care—how organizations can prioritize wellness and resilience within team structures. More specifically, team care involves operationalizing wellness practices within the current structure of job duties and routines, leading by example and showing transparency, creating time and space to support staff by talking about how the work impacts their emotional and physical health, referring to employee benefits as a resource, offering structured debriefings after critical incidents, and building workforce knowledge of wellness and resilience.

The third year began with some delay, but eventually, four cohorts participated in the research study and preliminary findings indicated decreased stress and improved wellness. Participants acknowledged difficulties in achieving parental resilience but learned information and skills that aided them in the process of strengthening resilience. A global pandemic adjusted the timeline for the study and created unprecedented challenges for participants, organizations, and communities. However, it also afforded new opportunities to focus on improved health and wellness.

Lessons Learned

A few professional and personal life lessons emerged over the three years working on this research project. First, the commitment that community-based partners must make to a research project should be well-planned, yet flexible because of the unpredictable nature of community-centered work. Having supportive colleagues and research partners can ease the process of navigating the successes and setbacks that arise with research projects. The key to creating and maintaining those supportive relationships seems to be communication. Regular, honest, clear, and courageous communication was helpful throughout the journey.

Secondly, the amount of trauma exposure professionals experience when working in community settings is profound and life-transforming. It sometimes jolts the professional into an immediate stress response and reactive stance, but it can also have a more subtle, chronic impact on day-to-day functioning. This trauma exposure has the potential to restate the importance of violence prevention work and align professionals with goals and passion to use their training and skills for the community or agency's benefit. But it takes a significant toll on the mind, body, and soul as well. Developing a lifestyle of wellness and finding ways to continually practice resilience and growth mindset are critical for the professional's health and career longevity.

Lastly, the positive impact that community-based research can have on individuals, families, and stakeholders is motivating. Involving community partners who are close to the issues and resources are vital to helping to create interventions, programs, or policies that can benefit the community. Establishing lasting university–community partnerships has the potential to create opportunities for meaningful collaboration and bring the community to the table to explore problems and solutions together.

Conclusion

This community-engaged research project was rewarding, yet overwhelming and stressful. Some challenges community partners face in community-engaged research include shifting agency priorities, protocols that involve colleagues unrelated to the research, and unexpected job changes. These can delay research timelines or cause barriers that require changes to the focus of the project. Perhaps the most overlooked and underestimated aspect of working with community partners is the emotional toll the work can take on an individual and how that impacts their time and energy to focus on research.

The natural stressors and setbacks that occur in life and in research offer the chance to flex growth mindset muscles and gain more sophisticated skills to not just *survive* adversity, but to *thrive*. Resilience must be woven into daily life through choices and habits that build upon one another. It also must transfer into the workplace to create cultures of organizational resilience. From there, communities can heal and become resilient places for all citizens to live and thrive.

References

Carver, C. S. (1998). Resilience and thriving: Issues, models, and linkages. *Journal of Social Issues, 54*, 245–266.

Center on the Developing Child (2015). *InBrief: The science of resilience.* https://developingchild.harvard.edu/wp-content/uploads/2015/05/InBrief-The-Science-of-Resilience.pdf

Dweck, C. (2008). *Mindset: The new psychology of success.* Random House Digital, Inc.

Gurwitch, R. H., Pfefferbaum, B., Montgomery, J. M., Klomp, R. W., & Reissman, D. B. (2007). *Building community resilience for children and families.* Terrorism and Disaster Center at the University of Oklahoma Health Sciences Center.

Masten, A. S. (2014). *Ordinary magic: Resilience in development.* Guilford Press.

McKeown, G. (2014) *Essentialism: The disciplined pursuit of less.* Crown Business.

Palmiter, D., Alvord, M., Dorlen, R., Comas-Diaz, L., Luthar, S., Maddi, S., O'Neill, H., Saakvitne, K. & Tedeschi, R. (2012). *Building your resilience.* American Psychological Association. https://www.apa.org/topics/resilience

Porter, L., Martin, K. & Anda, R. (2016). *Self-healing communities: A transformational process model for improving intergenerational health.* The Robert Wood Johnson Foundation. https://www.rwjf.org/en/library/research/2016/06/self-healing-communities.html

Rubin, G. (2015). *Better than before: Mastering the habits of our everyday lives.* Penguin Random House.

Schramm, D., Warzinik, K., Allen, J., Reese, C., Schreiber, K., Malzner, L. & Cunningham, P. (2017). *Strong parents, stable children: Building protective factors to strengthen families.* Missouri Foundation for Child Abuse Prevention. https://ctf4kids.org/wp-content/uploads/2015/07/SPSC_FOR-Web.pdf

Singleton, H. (2020). Shooting deaths remained high in Columbia this year during pandemic. https://www.columbiamissourian.com/news/local/shooting-deaths

-remained-high-in-columbia-this-year-during-pandemic/article_1ceb48be-3515-11eb-aab4-8347f6ce9939.html

Smith, B., Dalen, J., Wiggins, K., Tooley, E., Christopher, P. & Bernard, J. (2008). The brief resilience scale: Assessing the ability to bounce back. *International Journal of Behavioral Medicine*, *15*, 194–200.

Stamm, B. H. (2002). Measuring compassion satisfaction as well as fatigue: Developmental history of the compassion satisfaction and fatigue test. In C. R. Figley (Ed.), *Treating compassion fatigue,* (pp. 107–119). Brunner-Routledge.

Swarbrick, M. (2006) A wellness approach. *Psychiatric Rehabilitation Journal*, *29*(4), 311–314.

The International Consortium on Organizational Resilience (2016). *The community resilience framework.* https://www.build-resilience.org/community-resilience-framework.php

The International Consortium on Organizational Resilience (2016). *The organizational resilience model.* https://www.build-resilience.org/organizational-resilience-framework.php

van der Kolk, B. A. (2014). *The body keeps the score: Brain, mind, and body in the healing of trauma.* Viking.

Chapter 8

Researching Resilience

Collaboration and Critique Through Community Engagement

Clark M. Peters and Kelli E. Canada

The essays presented in this volume invite readers into a conversation about working with communities to understand how the concept of resilience can inform health research. As with any good conversation, the chapter authors weave in personal reflections as they provide insights into the challenges and rewards of working in true partnership with community members. Each author emphasizes the central importance of engaging with community members in exploring the contours of resilience, what it can illuminate, and how it can inform efforts to build a culture of health in communities. Across chapters, authors both celebrate and interrogate resilience in an effort to disrupt and reimagine the concept through a community-based participatory research (CBPR) lens. Resilience cannot be studied at arm's length; it requires full participation of people that traditional research calls "subjects," a term counterproductive in this context. Scholars, agency partners, and community members each bring essential ingredients to develop workable strategies, certainly, but also to shape the ways that key terms are defined and measured, which the authors recognize can be vague and at times very much contested.

As the introductory chapter notes, there is clearly ambiguity in the concept of risk, the challenges met with resilience. While scholars make claims to providing objective measures of risk, as we deepen our understanding of systemic oppression and personal and community trauma, we learn that circumstances can have different effects on different individuals and communities. Resilience offers a way to emphasize the strengths of those facing risk rather than just their deficits, but, as Chatman and Wright discuss in their chapter on building community with youths, and as Kheru notes in his chapter critiquing the concept of resilience, elevating resilience can also be problematic: doing so can insidiously rationalize deprivation, disregard larger forces at play, and absolve those in power from taking stronger action. Grit should be celebrated, but in the face of racism, violence, and oppression, it is inadequate without broader community action. Although resilience, as a construct, is critiqued in this volume, authors do recognize the need for reshaping and rethinking its meaning and application.

Ecological Nature of Resilience

As with resilience, however, defining "community" can also be challenging. The term is shorthand for different collections of individuals who share common interests, characteristics, proximity, history, faith, or values. Just listing these elements, however, invites oversimplification. In their chapter, Goodkind, Elliott, and Brinkman emphasize that intersectionality means that people are more than the sum of their traits. Moreover, in her discussion on youth resilience in Oakland, Jackson notes that each of these elements inject fluidity in how we understand membership; community members can come and go and shared attributes may change. Somehow, however, communities tend to retain an essential cohesion that can nevertheless blur in specifics (Chaskin, 1997).

In her argument for the need to change traditional medical research, Moore emphasizes that "community and individual resilience are inextricably intertwined," a message woven throughout this volume. In disentangling individual and community elements of the term, the authors provide an important insight into a hidden tension; resilience cannot be defined simply as stoic responses to difficult circumstances. Kheru notes in his critique of resilience that traditional framings of resilience tend to blame individuals for the disadvantages they face, so that anything short of complete acceptance of one's disadvantage indicates irresponsibility. However, other chapter authors emphasize that in oppressive contexts oppositional behavior is often adaptive, even as activism against oppression may be seen as provocative, hostile, and inimical to healthy prosocial behavior. Using the Black Girls Advocacy and Leadership Alliance as an example, Goodkind, Elliott, and Brinkman note that such behavior, especially when expressed by people of color, is often characterized as delinquent and dangerous. Sometimes, expressions of resilience are met with punishment. By recognizing the ecological nature of resilience, we can reduce its inherent tension and cultivate resilience among both individuals and communities. The project Goodkind, Elliott, and Brinkman describe shows how collaborating to understand the nature of oppression can be empowering, and how leveraging internal resilience to build external action can strengthen individuals and reduce risk simultaneously.

Researchers and scholars also need to reexamine the study of these topics and avoid oversimplification. Too often, risk is quantified as the sum of individual deprivation, disregarding the multiplicative nature of risk factors and the broad ecological factors at play. Researchers must acknowledge that resilience is recognized in individuals facing challenges only, as Kheru notes, "because so many others have failed." Communities are more than a collection of individuals; they also comprise organizations, including human service agencies, informal associations, and faith-based institutions. These organizations, in turn, include community members, but as Jones points out in her chapter on personal resilience when engaging in research, it is important to recognize organizations as members unto themselves. She emphasizes the need to pay mind to organizational resilience and supportive work environments that encourage healthy practices for individual members and the broader community. An essential element of this work is self-care; depleted organizations facing large caseloads, high turnover, and inadequate professional supervision will not be productive community members.

Power, Trust, and Diversity in Perspective

The compilation of chapters in this volume take place in this complex, ambiguous, exciting, and fraught context. The authors—researchers engaged with communities and community members engaged in research—seek to shed light on how we can improve the nature of inquiry into sticky social problems to inform and improve health outcomes through community-engaged research. Chatman and Wright note that community-engaged research requires collaboration that brings community members together, and they are likely to have distinct opinions about their circumstances. But collectively, their insights and recommendations may provide a distinct path for how to move forward toward building more resilient communities and, ultimately, reducing the risk that necessitates resilience in the first place. As different as the voices are, there are common threads throughout the volume regarding critical issues for health research: power, trust, and diversity of perspectives.

Power

Power is inevitably a dynamic in the research enterprise, and especially so in understanding resilience. Research, and the people involved, are fundamentally political. Through the research process, people define what is important and what is not, as well as the nature of relationships connecting relevant variables. These questions and terms of the research may be influenced, if not dictated, by funders, and the auspice of the research affects the manner of investigation and protocols for disseminating findings. The story told by research is often unexamined by research participants, along with assumptions and biases. Even when authors acknowledge distinct voices from the communities they study, inevitably, they must select which voices get heard, and which are ignored. While it is comforting to think that data can speak for itself, even in the most strictly quantitative research, it rarely can. Research inevitably involves data reduction—summarizing and selecting data to find meaning—but recognizing the subjectivity inherent in research, including community-engaged research, does not undermine the rigor or methods germane to good social inquiry. Kheru notes that researchers see themselves as positive forces, contributing to knowledge, and certainly not engaged in harming communities. Good intentions, of course, are no guarantee of positive outcomes. However, failing to understand the context in which the studies take place, Moore notes, as well as the inherent power imbalances between research institutions and the disadvantaged communities they study, will undermine the credibility of any findings.

One important way that scholars, researchers, and professionals maintain their power over domains of knowledge is through establishing expertise. While scientists will honestly represent their goal as seeking to expand understanding of the world we are in, they also must work to establish their credibility as masters of their respective fields. Socialization within each academic subfield involves learning the relevant norms and jargon, as well as the distinguishing characteristics that make each subfield, in its own way, uniquely advantaged over other fields. Chatman and Wright bemoan the siloed nature of academic fields that overlap in topics but are separated by distinct terminology and disconnected journals and conferences. Such socialization is also evident among professions seeking recognition and respect (Abbott, 1988), and builds on the rigid Eurocentric educational process criticized by Kheru.

A number of this volume's authors note the power in knowledge and the dangers of research institutions positioning themselves as arbiters of truth and brokers of that knowledge (e.g., see Kheru) particularly when studying concepts like resilience. Goodkind, Elliott, and Brinkman once again note the possibilities of this equation: If research leads to knowledge and knowledge is power, and if resilience is a demonstration of power, then research that engages community members can itself cultivate power and resilience directly. They emphasize that research leads to resilience only if researchers truly share the power they bring (Alang, Batts, & Letcher, 2020). Once again, however, research institutions tend to make power-sharing difficult. Their own authority lies in their claims to expertise and knowledge, reinforced by resources, titles, arcane processes, and jargon. Further complicating these conversations is that, as Jackson notes in her account of being the community partner in research projects, each field has its own unique language, further raising the barriers to participation for non-academic community members.

Power and Participation

The authors in this volume note the irony of researchers who visit communities with good intentions but sometimes dubious claims of expertise and communication tools that are designed to certify expertise as much as they are to explain complicated concepts. Scholars may bring an inflated sense of the importance of their work and the willingness of community and agency partners to contribute. Community partners take risks participating in research and as Jones, a community-based clinician, suggests, often use their personal time to do so. Communities do this, however, with the hope for change or a contribution to the development of new knowledge. Unfortunately, as Moore notes, far too many communities who are hard at work as research subjects will never see, participate in dissemination, or ultimately benefit from the results of the research they took part in.

Over the last several years, public health and select social sciences have argued against "parachute research," which is defined by *The Lancet Global Health* editorial board (2018) as "one who drops into a country, makes use of the local infrastructure, personnel, and patients, and then goes home and writes an academic paper for a prestigious journal." More broadly, this metaphor is a criticism of scholars who intersect with communities they seek to study, extract information, vanish, and publish findings in outlets typically unavailable to the research subjects. Moore argues that this method of research is not only limiting in value to communities but, more importantly, exploitive. Moore suggests that part of power sharing should be in concrete resources; community members should be fairly compensated for their contribution to research financially, and research activities should employ community labor to the extent possible. In addition to the obvious need to financially compensate community members, there is also a need for shared decision-making with community partners about the research and collaborative writing of papers for academic journals—an act that can and does build community resilience and power.

Community-engaged research demands engagement with the community that does not end abruptly at the end of the research period. Community-engaged research does become personal; researchers may even become a part of the community. As Jackson reflects, the end of a research project doesn't necessarily bring that membership with a community to an end or absolve responsibilities one has to community members. Sharing power means that the researchers do not have the right to grab the data and decide when and how to use it. Jones notes that sharing what scholars know, the aims of the research, and key findings is no easy feat, even if done skillfully. Dissemination tends to be the final stage for researchers, and Moore notes that a strategy should be developed in the initial plans to speed absorption of information into communities throughout the research process. Rather than protecting and restricting access to knowledge, both new and old, until the project's end, sharing research findings is best done provisionally throughout the research period and in collaboration with the community. Authors emphasize the importance of deploying alternative means of collecting information and conveying complex concepts. In their respective chapters, Jackson, and Chatman and Wright offer important examples of how hip hop, poetry, and visual arts can provide means to tell the essential stories of a community and reflect back the results of the research work; doing so must be done in close collaboration with community members. Kheru recognizes that some information cannot be conveyed in any other way.

Trust

In building trust and credibility in the context of community-engaged research, research inevitably becomes a matter of personal relationships. In a real sense, researchers become members of the community, if only provisionally and bounded. Good research in this context requires collaboration with community members, who in turn become part of the research enterprise (provisionally and bounded, as well). As Goodkind, Elliott, and Brinkman argue, trust requires *involvement*. The best path to building trust and thus, solid research findings, as Moore suggests, might not always be a direct one; non-research or so-called unrelated activities (e.g., volunteering, helping set up activities) may actually be essential to building capacity for the research and establishing trust. As Jackson suggests, membership in the community by researchers is helpful; however, trust can be built with outsiders with intentional and genuine effort as well as acknowledgment of historical exploitations, as Moore argues. Key components to building trust are authenticity, humility, and showing care for the community.

When researchers have not built trust with their community, the impact can be extensive. One example of how trust, or a lack of trust, may impact the research process is through recruitment efforts. Chatman and Wright, as well as Jones, discuss the common challenge of recruitment in research in their respective chapters, but when trust has not been established, recruitment efforts are even more problematic. Researchers often express dismay at their struggles to recruit study participants and at the mistrust expressed by communities they study. However, in community-engaged research, representatives of communities are the most knowledgeable about how to build trust in the research, where to recruit, and how to recruit. This kind of capacity building for the research may involve months of meeting people, talking about the work, and gathering myriad perspectives to develop a plan that works for the unique community involved in the research.

Not all researchers will be naturally comfortable with the personal nature of community-engaged research, and indeed, it runs counter to the objectivity often presumed to be germane to rigorous research. Such professional distance, however, disregards the high stakes of health outcomes that researchers examine and the very real consequences for community members. As Jackson notes, it is disingenuous to disregard the personal nature of the work. Chatman and Wright emphasize, however, that concerns of entanglement with community does not necessarily compromise the rigor required of good research, so long as investigators are self-reflective. Self-reflection must go hand-in-hand with the passion and engagement required of ethical and rigorous community-engaged research, and also helps to reduce any potential bias introduced from researchers' own personal experiences.

Jones recognizes the difficult balance needed between establishing professional boundaries and detachment from the work; good research and personal care require that investigators maintain some equilibrium. Research on resilience requires all partners to pay mind to self-care, Jones argues. Compassion fatigue (i.e., feeling emotionally drained from the work) and compassion satisfaction (i.e., the rewards from the work itself) both fuel the bonds between all members of the research team. Building a foundation of trust requires researchers to recognize, experience, and respond to the emotional components of the research process that are often ignored or controlled in more traditional approaches to research. Jones suggests that as teams feel and experience together, building space for celebrating and grieving is essential.

Diversifying Research Perspectives

In involving community team members, community-engaged research features a diverse team. The composition of that team, however, must be carefully considered. Kheru emphasizes the need to encourage disagreement to find otherwise-unrecognized opportunities to plan the research. He also offers a solution for the problem of having research jargon and processes inhibit honest discussion; he encourages discussions among community participants without researchers present. Jones notes that organizational and professional members of the community have different roles that may be bound by contractual terms, professional obligations, and agency expectations. That is to say, these participants do not always speak with one voice, and separate discussions will allow differences, as well as novel solutions, to emerge.

The need to diversify the research enterprise, however, is not limited to research projects. Authors in this volume of work suggest that normative change is needed throughout the research process, including the composition and practice of academic bodies with authority over research activities. Contemporary research is generally subject to oversight for purposes of human subjects' protection. Institutional Review Boards (IRBs) at universities, state agencies, and research institutions, however, do not guarantee safe or ethical research. Before any university-based research project begins, it must receive approval from the relevant IRB at the sponsoring institution. The IRB review seeks to ensure the protection of human subjects by terminating or revising unnecessarily risky projects and those unlikely to yield benefits that outweigh the risks to participants. Emerging from tragic and unconscionable medical experiments conducted in the name of science, human subject protections are now extended far beyond the field of medicine. Even before the rise of the internet, advocates recognized the dangers of releasing private information that could cause tremendous harm to research participants emotionally, socially, and economically.

Moore notes that harm, even if it is outweighed by research benefits, is far more likely to land on studies involving people of color and residents of poor communities. IRBs do recognize the potential of coercion, for example, limiting compensation to research subjects so they will not be unduly compelled to participate for money. However, IRBs often overlook that fairness demands that individuals and communities be compensated fairly for their time and expertise. IRBs also do not recognize other power imbalances, such as those between the university and the community itself. IRBs will often include in cost–benefit calculations the potential contributions of research to knowledge-building, relying on general altruism on the part of recipients. The return to the researcher tends not to be included or acknowledged. IRBs generally include at least one representative of the community, broadly defined. Typically, this member adds racial, cultural, or topical diversity to the board and may indeed bring a distinct perspective. In practice, however, the community voice is difficult to assert into the context of research administration. Moore rejects the view of research that the objects of study are no more than human subjects and warns against reclassifying their participation as simply actions within a study. Most research, as well as IRB oversight, follows a traditional medical model and tends to have a narrow individual focus. Moore notes, however, that health outcomes are mostly a function of nonmedical factors; demoting community-level factors in favor of an individual-level focus is short-sighted, if not simply wrongheaded.

Beyond the IRB supervision, university-based researchers generally face a strict and limited measure of success: publication in high-impact, peer-reviewed journals. Scientific ideas, the assumption goes, ought to face the scrutiny of colleagues, typically anonymously, and approval of editors. If these ideas, expressed in manuscripts that are submitted to academic journals, are deemed worthy for publication, the author is rewarded with recognition and increased likelihood of receiving the rewards of promotion and tenure. The process, however, is deeply flawed. Kheru and Jackson note that the process requires that the steps involved with peer review, the de facto legitimization of research, is largely conducted by White and male professionals, who may not entertain ideas that challenge Eurocentric approaches to research questions or have respect for the nonlinear process of community-engaged research.

Community-engaged research requires flexibility and time, characteristics that Chatman and Wright note can be at odds against traditional research expectations. Working to co-create knowledge with communities tends to be unpredictable and nonlinear. Goodkind, Elliott, and Brinkman advise that researchers bring humility and a willingness to change research plans. As other researchers noted, community-oriented research needs to start with observation; entering communities armed with research questions will guarantee that those questions will almost certainly be the wrong ones (Venkatesh, 2002). Taking the time to infuse diverse community and research perspectives into each phase of the research is far more likely to produce beneficial research to address complex social problems. Yet, the recommendations of this volume's authors are in tension with the academic context most researchers inhabit.

Conclusion

The authors in this volume have a number of important suggestions for those engaging in research on resilience in communities, and few are modest. Just as Goodkind, Elliott, and Brinkman encourage challenging norms regarding Black girls, the authors recognize that the tremendous inertia of the modern research enterprise will require systemic changes. Kheru notes that Eurocentric assumptions limit the way we even engage in scholarly debate. As the norms that led to today's gross inequalities are challenged, acknowledging that prevailing perspectives suppress competing realities requires recognition. This recognition and subsequent reform may offer communities a future that is more just and fair in their participation in the enterprise of research. Drawing on African traditions, Kheru offers the Structured Dialogue method as a way out of this iron cage to emphasize vulnerability and equality among discussants.

Chatman and Wright note that scholarship tends to be siloed, each field and subfield with distinct accreditations, conferences, journals, and professional networks. A successful academic career path often involves identifying a narrow research path and allows specialization in a distinct area or field of study. Such emphasis, however, undervalues competing viewpoints, including multicultural interpretations of concepts like resilience. Chatman and Wright acknowledge that change is likely to be slow, but warn that in working within current structures, there is a danger of reinforcing existing inequalities. They also note the ironic tradition of social researchers to implicitly or explicitly criticize community culture—of poverty, of families of color—but decline to examine the culture of academic communities.

Authors express hope, as we do, that the next generation of scholars and community members will have a broader understanding of scholarship and the need to involve communities in the research that affects them. Jackson; Chatman and Wright; and Goodkind, Elliott, and Brinkman all note the importance of involving young people in research, as they will become our next community leaders, agency directors, and university scholars. Rather than socializing these young people in centuries-old traditions of academia and exclusively Eurocentric scientific norms, we should encourage them to question the foundations of knowledge. Doing so will ensure that they bring the skepticism and innovation to build new norms in research, including ones that identify and value the role of community-engaged research in building community resilience and a culture of health, as well as generating an inclusive knowledge base.

References

Abbott, A. (1988). *The system of professions: An essay on the division of expert labor.* University of Chicago Press.

Alang, S., Batts, H., & Letcher, A. (2020). Interrogating academic hegemony in community-based participatory research to address health inequities. *Journal of Health Services Research & Policy*, 26(3), pp. 215–220. https://doi.org/10.1177/1355819620963501.

Chaskin, R. J. (1997). Perspectives on neighborhood and community: A review of the literature. *Social Service Review*, 71(4), 521–547. https://www.journals.uchicago.edu/doi/abs/10.1086/604277

The Lancet Global Health Editorial Board (2018). Closing the door on parachutes and parasites. *Lancet*, 6(6), eS93. https://doi.org/10.1016/S2214-109X(18)30239-0

Venkatesh, S. A. (2002). *American project: The rise and fall of a modern ghetto.* Harvard University Press.

Bios

Volume editor bios

Kelli E. Canada, PhD, LCSW, is an Associate Professor at the University of Missouri—Columbia, School of Social Work. She worked more than 15 years in social work in direct services and administration. Canada's research focuses on interventions for people with mental illnesses who become involved in the criminal–legal system, including community interventions, alternative sentencing, and programming within institutions using mixed methods and community-engaged approaches. She also examines the policies and practices impacting recidivism and quality of life of people formerly incarcerated. Canada is an alumnus of the Robert Wood Johnson Foundation Interdisciplinary Research Leader program.

Clark Peters, PhD, MSW, JD, an Associate Professor at the University of Missouri School of Social Work and Truman School of Government and Public Affairs, focuses his work primarily on child welfare, adolescents in state care, and juvenile justice. He has presented, taught, and written widely on issues of juvenile justice, foster care, and child welfare. His current research focuses on youths transitioning from foster care, family court supervision of child welfare, and elevating community-engaged research in academic settings.

Contributor bios

Britney G. Brinkman, PhD, is an interdisciplinary researcher and an Associate Professor of Psychology. She works with schools and community organizations to promote justice for girls. She is the recipient of a Citizen Psychologist Presidential Citation from the American Psychological Association.

Michelle C. Chatman, PhD, is Associate Professor of Criminal Justice at the University of the District of Columbia (UDC). She is a cultural anthropologist committed to Black family wellbeing, youth justice, and contemplative liberatory pedagogy. She is an alumna of Interdisciplinary Research Leaders Cohort 2.

Kathi R. Elliott, DNP, MSW, PMHNP-BC, is the CEO of Gwen's Girls, a nonprofit that provides holistic programs to girls. Dr. Elliott is a psychiatric nurse practitioner with years of experience in social service, and community and individual mental health treatment.

Sara Goodkind, PhD, MSW, is Associate Professor of Social Work, Sociology, and Gender, Sexuality, and Women's Studies at the University of Pittsburgh. Goodkind's research focuses on social service programs and systems that work with young people—tracing young people's pathways, examining institutional biases and inequities, and providing evidence and recommendations for systems and policy change.

Regina Jackson is a global thought leader for youth development. For the past 27 years, she has served as President and CEO of the East Oakland Youth Development Center. Jackson served as a Robert Wood Johnson Foundation Interdisciplinary Research Fellow from 2017 to 2020.

Rachel Jones, MEd, LPC, is a licensed professional counselor specializing in trauma. She received a master's degree in Educational, School, and

Counseling Psychology, and a bachelor's degree in Sociology and minor in Black Studies from the University of Missouri-Columbia.

Jomo Kheru is a media psychologist invested in African liberation. He is founder and Executive Director at Jomoworks, and has over 15 years of faculty and administrative experience in university teaching and learning, faculty governance, and social and instructional media.

Quianta Moore, MD, JD, is an action-oriented researcher who partners with communities to co-create a research agenda that identifies challenges and actionable solutions to effectuate change. Dr. Moore is the Executive Director of the Hackett Center for Mental Health at Meadows Mental Health Policy Institute and a Fellow in Child Health Policy at Rice University's Baker Institute for Public Policy.

Ryan T. Wright, MA, LGPC, is a licensed graduate professional counselor from Washington, D.C., where he works as an intake coordinator and mental health therapist. Wright aims to utilize mindfulness and humanistic theory and practice to help others heal holistically.

Index

f refers to figure; *n* refers to footnote

A
abuse
  by police, 27, 37, 67, 80
  by research industry, 79–80
  research triggering memories of, 146
academic journals
  Dill and Jackson publish in, 144
  Jackson and Fong-Gomez publish in, 151
  and parachute research, 189
  on problems in disseminating knowledge, 188
  for research and funding opportunities, 76
  researchers' publication in, 136, 194–95
  and sharing information with community, 190
  on trauma-informed care, 175
accountability, 82, 85
action research. *see* community-based participatory research (CBPR)
Addae, Kofi, 120
addictions and recovery, 160
Adinkra symbol, 118
Adkins, Rachelle, 64
African American communities.
  differences in learning, *vs.* White, 125
  in District of Columbia, 63
  effect of long-term stressors upon, 6
  and lack of trust in health care system, 80
  loss of history and culture in, 88
  see also Neighborhood A (case study); Neighborhood B case study)

African/Black psychology in the American context (Kambon), 119
African culture
  basis of SDM, 114–17
  contributions to science and math ignored, 108
  vs. European, 124–25
  proficiency in, for research team members, 10
Afrika, Laila, 120–21
after-school jobs, 57
Allegheny Co., Pittsburgh, PA
  Department of Human Services, 17
  Elliott's hometown, 30
  see also Black Girls Advocacy and Leadership Alliance (BGALA); Black Girls Equity Alliance (BGEA)
Allen, J., 7, 194
Alston, Sharon T., 42, 53–54, 70*n*
altruism, 82, 194
Alvarado, Manuel, 70*n*
ambiguity, 6–7, 184
American Public Health Association (APHA), 143, 144, 149
Anderson, L., 1, 6
Ani, M. (Richards), 121
anthropology, 43, 48
Arbery, Ahmaud, 47
Aristotle, 108
arts
  as part of Project Youth MIND, 42, 43, 45, 60, 190
  as research component of EOYDC, 138
  visual, 190

Asili (seed of culture), 124
awareness *vs.* observing, 59
"A Wellness Approach," 172

B
Backyard Band, 63
Bacon, Francis, 108
Baldwin, James, 111
banking education, 116, 123
behavior
   in disenfranchised communities, 132
   and gender norms, 59–60
   impact of Covid-19 on behavior studies, 176
   oppositional, as adaptive, 185
   prosocial, 94
   research with drug fenfluramine, 80
Behavioral Medicine, 26
Belmont Report, 79–80, 81
Biden, Joe, 37
Bishop O'Dowd High School, 145
Black feminism, 23, 26, 48
Black Girls Advocacy and Leadership Alliance (BGALA)
   evaluation of initial year, 26–28
   and incorporation into BGEA, 15
   IRL support for, 15, 22, 29, 32
   lessons learned, 32–36
   and oppositional behavior, 185
   program design, 25–26
   "River of Life" activity, 29–32, *30*
   theory and values guiding, 21–25
   three founders of, 9
Black Girls Equity Alliance (BGEA)
   founding and purpose of, 15, 16–21
   report on juvenile justice in Allegheny Co., 37
Black history, 26
Black Lives Matter movement, 9
Black Panthers, 137

Black psychology, 10, 119, 124–25
body scanning, 56, 60
bomb threats, 156
Bowser, Muriel, 61
brain development, 54, 57–58, 64, 68, 168
Brinkman, Britney G.
   background of, 31
   on challenging norms of Black girls, 196
   flexibility in research, 195
   and Gwen's Girls, 19, 36
   on intersectionality, 184
   involving young people in research, 196
   on oppositional behavior, 185
   partnership with BGALA, 9, 33, 35–36
   on power sharing, 188
   on trust and involvement, 191–92
Brown, Adrienne Maree, 35
Brown students
   adversity among, 126
   effect of Eurocentrism in education upon, 108, 111
   gaining trust in, 147
   identity development in, 145
Bryant, Kobe, 106*n,* 106–7
Buddhism, 50
bullying, 31, 65
bus tickets, 25
Buzz (numbers game), 55

C
California, University of
   Berkeley Graduate School of Public Health, 144, 145
   Berkeley-UCSF Joint Medical Program, 145
   SF Benioff Children's Hospital, 150
California Endowment, 132, 134
California State Department of Education, 125
caregivers, 159, 174

Carruthers, J. H., 108
carryover effect, 111
cars, 92
case studies of African American neighborhoods, 84–92
CashApp prizes, 64
cellphones
    to attend Project Youth MIND sessions, 66–67
    as distractions, 56
Centers for Disease Control (CDC), 98
Charlton, James, 12
Chatman, Michelle
    on arts and community, 190
    on collaboration, 186
    on involving young people in research, 59, 196
    limitations of academic scholarships, 196
    on mindfulness and meditation, 48–50, 56, 59
    on problematic nature of resilience, 184
    on siloed nature of academic fields, 188
    as team member of Project Youth MIND, 9, 42, 48–50, 52–54, 59
    on time constraints in research, 195
    on trust and recruitment, 191–92
child welfare system, 18, 160
Christmas, 72
Clifton, Lucille, 64
Coghill, Abdullah R., 48
collective identity, 28
Collins, Patricia Hill, 20
Common Rule, 80
communication
    in CBPR research, 11, 34, 62, 64, 93, 112
    as central principle of CBPR, 5
    and FCDI, 112
    key to supportive relationships, 178
    misleading, 163, 189
    nonviolent, 64, 68
    to stakeholders, 157
    structured dialogue method as, 10, 114, 118
communities
    case studies of African American neighborhoods, 84–92
    different descriptions of, 5
    importance of resilience in, 76–77
    violence in, 65
Community Advisory Boards (CAB), 89, 91, 93, 94, 95, 97
community agreements, 65
community-based participatory research (CBPR)
    academic support needed for, 36
    alternative definitions of, 2
    case studies, 84–92
    central principles of, 4–5, 92
    from community member's perspective, 11
    and creating accountability, 82
    decentralization of research process, 36
    flexibility necessary component of, 35
    influence upon founding of BGEA, 21
    relationships and trust central to, 9
    rooted in social justice, 5
    value and recognition of, 98
community development, 76
community-engaged research. *see* community-based participatory research (CBPR)
community members and financial compensation to, 189, 194
Community Resilience Framework, 160
compassion fatigue and satisfaction, 160, 192
computers
    access to, 67
    lack of access to, 61–62

concision, 117
conference participation, 136, 188
confidentiality, 163, 169
consent
    as ethical principle, 80
    and financial incentives, 81
    lack of, in Henrietta Lacks' case, 79
    from parents, 62
Cooper, Gary, 112
counters (objections to ideas), 117
Covid-19 pandemic
    and African Americans' lack of trust in healthcare, 80
    effect on Project Youth MIND, 9, 43, 47, 61
    and grant dollars' distribution, 96
    impact upon holidays and family gatherings, 72
    impact upon Jones's research, 174, 175–77
    impact upon marginalized communities, 36, 67
    impact upon self-care, 176–78
    use of Zoom meetings during, 37
crack epidemic, 48
Crenshaw, Kimberlé, 17, 20
crime
    criminal records, 92
    and impact upon community resilience, 78
critical race theory, 36
crystal bowl meditation, 56, 60
culture
    African cultural basis of SDM, 114–17
    African *vs.* European, 124–25
    Asili (seed of), 124
    of Black D. C. communities, 63
    Chatman's interest in, 49
culture of health
    focus of RWJF, 3, 22, 155
    resilience necessary for, 159
    role of medical research in, 75
    use of CBPR to advance, 8–9, 12
    see also specific projects
Curry, T., 109

D
Darwin, Charles, 106
data sharing, 96, 187
Davis, Angela, 137
Davis, Sandra, 134
"Death of White Research in the Black Community," (Williams), 110
deaths
    Curry on death of Black males, 109
    due to Covid-19, 67, 80, 177
    homicide as form of trauma, 156
    homicide rates in Oakland, 134–35, 135n
    homicides during Jones's research, 164–65, 170, 175
debit cards, 25
debriefing sessions, 57, 65, 165, 177
decision fatigue, 166
decision-making
    empowered, 139, 146, 188–89
    and SDM, 113
    shared, 19, 83–85, 88–89, 91–92
deep breathing, 59
dialogue, 114–17, 121
digital divide, 66–68
Dill, LeConte, 134–39, 143–44, 148, 152
disability rights movement, 12, 20
disagreement, 10, 125–26
disaster research, 76
Disciplined Pursuit of Less, The, (McKeown), 166
disease "hotspots," 90
distance-learning courses, 157, 162
District of Columbia

Department of Parks and Recreation
(DCDPR), 54–58, 61–64, 160
Go-Go music workshops, 63
segregation and digital divide in, 66–68
District of Columbia, University of
(UDC), 42
diversion programs, 18
documentation, 136, 138
domestic violence, 156, 160
dress code violations, 27, 28
drug dens, 140
drug rehab counselors, 64
drug use, 132
Duncan, Ajeenah, 70*n*

E
East Oakland Building Healthy
Communities initiative (EOBHC),
132
East Oakland Youth Development Center
(EOYDC)
first session, 138–40
former students as presenters at APHA,
143
homicide rates in Oakland, 134–35,
135*n*
identity development project for young
men of color, 145–50
Jackson on CBPR from community
member's perspective, 11, 131–34,
188
Jackson's collaboration with Dill,
134–39, 143–44, 148, 152
project as path to resilience, 135–45
project results, 140–42
as safe space, 140–42
as site of "Portrait Project" gallery
show, 150
eating, 59–60
ecology, 1, 7, 42, 76, 184–86

economic mobility, 88
editors, 195
education
banking system of, 116, 123
from HBCU, 134
racial trauma embedded in, 10, 108–12
role of Black psychology in, 10, 119,
124–25
using SDM, 114–17
Egyptians, 108
Elliott, Gwendolyn J.
founder of Gwen's Girls, 30
on intersectionality, 184
on oppositional behavior, 185
on power sharing, 188 30
Elliott, Kathi
background of, 29–31
as CEO of Gwen's Girls, 30
on challenging norms of Black girls,
196
on flexibility in research, 195
and Gwen's Girls, 18–19, 30
on involving young people in research,
196
partnership with BGALA, 9, 32
on trust and involvement, 191
emails
in designing Youth MIND, 52
lack of access to, and parental consent,
62
to mail poems, 64
emergency response, 160
*Emergent Strategy: Shaping Change,
Changing Worlds* (Brown), 35
employment
after-school jobs, 57
loss of, 80
and mental health interventions, 160
engineering, 76
Equity Summit, 18

"Eschatological Dilemma: The Problem of Studying the Black Male Only as the Deaths That Result from Anti-Black Racism" (Curry), 109
essentialism, 166, 168–69
ethics in medical research, 10, 79–84, 157, 193–94
Euclid, 108
Eurocentrism
    effect on peer review, 195
    effect upon education, 108, 111, 188
    effect upon scholarly research, 7, 195–97
    and victimization, 103
expulsions from school, 43

F
Facilitated Community Dialogues Initiative (FCDI), 112–13
"Failure of the Black Intellectual, The," (Frazier), 110
faith-based organizations. *see* religion and spirituality
family group conferences, 43
family unit, 8
federal agencies, 78. *see also specific agencies*
federal funding, 36–37
feedback sessions, 65
feminism, Black, 23, 26, 26. 48, 48
fenfluramine, 80
finance
    compensation to community members, 189, 194
    lack of financial opportunities, 78
finger snaps, 65
501 (c) 3 status, 95
Floyd, George, 37, 47
flyers, 168, 170, 173
Fong-Gomez, Stephanie, 145–52
Food and Drug Administration, U. S., 80
food deserts, 78
football, 32
Frazier, E. Franklin, 110
Freire, P, 114–15, 123
"from surviving to thriving," 159, 179–80
funders and funding opportunities
    and nonprofits, 135
    and power in research, 187
    sharing resources with community, 76, 83–84, 96–97

G
Gambia, The, 48
gang violence, 132
Garvey, John, 120
GED program, 148
gender norms, 59
gentrification, 67, 85–86, 88, 94
geometry, 108
Ghana, 118
Glover, Antwan "Big G," 63, 70*n*
gloves, protective, 63
Go-Go music, 63, 68, 70*n*
Goodkind, Sara
    background of, 30–32
    on challenging norms regarding Black girls, 196
    on flexibility in research, 195
    and Gwen's Girls, 19, 36
    on intersectionality, 184
    on involving young people in research, 196
    on oppositional behavior, 185
    partnership with BGALA, 9, 33
    on power sharing, 188
    studies referrals to juvenile justice system, 17
    on trust and involvement, 191
gossiping, 65
Graham, Dr. (pseudonym), 52–53
Graham, Philip, 151

Green, Joseph, 57, 64, 70*n*
grocery stores, 168
group discussions, 64, 146
Gwendolyn J. Elliott Institute (GJEI), 18–19, 36
Gwen's Girls
  founding of, 16, 30
  and Gwendolyn J. Elliott Institute, 18–19, 36
  recruitment of girls for BGALA, 25–26
  webinars, 37

H
habit pairing, 177
Hacker, K., 4–5
Harvard University. The Center for the Developing Child, 158
Hawkins, Miracle, 70*n*
healing spaces, 71
Henderson, Ronald Davon, 70*n*
Hilliard, A. G., 125
hip-hop, 45, 60, 190
Hippocratic Oath, 108
historically Black colleges and universities (HBCU), 134
HIV epidemic, 89
"hood beef," 65
Hotep, U, 118, 120, 121, 122
housing, 113, 160
  home ownership, in case study, 87
  inadequate, 78, 94
  safe and affordable, 3, 92, 93
Huxtables, the (TV family), 108
Hylton, K. Ivy, 42, 52, 56, 63, 70*n*

I
"I have kept what I have seen.", *mate matsie,* 118
Ichile, Iyelli, 70*n*
identify development project, 145–50
"I Live on a Block" (poem), 141
I.M.A.G.E. Camp summer program, 54–55, 64
Imhotep Student Interdisciplinary Research Conference (1999), 104
incentives
  financial for community participation, 90, 92
  and high risk of harm to research participants, 83
  for research, 81
Indigenous communities, 7
Inequities Affecting Black Girls in Pittsburgh and Allegheny County, 18
info graphics, 91
Instagram, 65, 65*n*
Institutional Review Board (IRB)
  in designing Project Youth MIND, 53, 61
  Dill submits IRB application, 144
  funds study of fenfluramine, 80
  Jackson secures IRB approval, 148
  for Jones's research projects, 158, 162, 169, 171
  oversight of academic research, 193–94
  on power imbalances between researcher and participants, 81, 96
intellectual disobedience, 119–20
intellectual maroonage
  intellectual disobedience, 119–20
  Jehewty on, 118
  liberational logic, 122–24
  Nyansa nnsa da, 120–22
"Intellectual Maroons: Architects of African Sovereignty," (Hotep), 118
Interdisciplinary Research Leaders (IRL). *see* Robert Wood Johnson Foundation (RWJF). Interdisciplinary Research Leaders (IRL)

International Consortium of
    Organizational Resilience, 160
internet, 194
intersectionality theory, 20–21, 141, 184
interviews, 139, 145, 176
involuntary leg movement, 104

J
Jackson, Noah, 145
Jackson, Regina
  on arts and community, 190
  on CBPR from community member's
    perspective, 11, 131–34, 188
  on changing nature of community,
    184–85
  collaboration with Dill, 134–39, 143–44,
    148, 152
  collaboration with Fong-Gomez,
    145–52
  collaboration with Madsen and
    Graham, 151–52
  on involving young people in research,
    196
  on limitations of peer review, 195
  as presenter at APHA, 143, 144
  on sharing research findings
    throughout project, 190
  on trust issues with community, 192
  on vetting researchers, 11, 136, 146, 152
Jacquez, F., 4
Ja'Keemah (college student), 142–43
Jay-Z, 103
Jeffersons, The (TV show), 108
Jehewty, Jedi Shemsu, 118
job opportunities
  creating new, 95
  joblessness in disenfranchised
    communities, 132
Jones, Rachel
  background as clinician, 156–57

basis of research project, 157–58
on CBPR from community member's
  perspective, 11, 155
on diversification in research, 193
on establishing boundaries, 192
on organizations and community
  members, 186
on resilience, 158–61
on time constrains for community
  partners, 189
on trust and recruitment, 191
year one of research project, 161–67
year two of research project, 167–73
year three of research project, 173–78
Journal of Adolescent Research, 151
Journal of Negro Education, 125
Jumper-Reeves, L., 7
juvenile justice system
  and mental health intervention, 160
  racial disparities in Pittsburgh, 17–18
  trauma-informed policies in, 174
  unethical research in, 80
  and violence prevention for Black girls,
    22–23

K
Kahoot! (trivia game), 67
Kambon, K. K., 119
Karenga, Maulana, 122
Keith, Tony, Jr., 70n
Kemetic yoga, 63, 70n
Kheru, Jomo
  on complexities of term "resilience," 10,
    184–86
  on disagreement and diversification, 193
  on Eurocentric educational process, 188
  on importance of arts, 190
  on limitations of peer review, 195
  on personal experiences of resilience,
    104–5, 109

on researchers as positive forces, 187
on Structured Dialogue method, 10, 196
Kikongo, 118
Korea. *see* South Korea
Krzyzewski, Mike, 106, 106*n*
Kwanzaa, 72

L

Lacks, Henrietta, 79
Lancet Global Health, The, 189
language
    Black *vs.* White differences in learning, 125
    socialization and academic jargon, 188
Latino and Latinx community
    Fong-Gomez's research into, 146–49
    importance of family unit for, 8
laundromats, 168
law enforcement, 160. *see also* police
Lebanon, 50–51
Lewis, Jason, 63, 70*n*
liberational logic, 122–24
literature
    on financial incentives for research participation, 81
    on lack of trust in healthcare during pandemic, 80
    on project success and resilience, 96
    on risk and resilience, 7
    and structured dialogue, 115
    see also academic journals
Long, Labrina, 56, 70*n*
Lonnell (pseudonym), 57

M

Maafa (African holocaust), 109
MA'AT Training Institute for Restorative Justice, 42
Madsen, Kris, 151–52
Mambo, Michelle, 17
masks, 61, 63, 72
Massachusetts Institute of Technology (MIT), 86, 87
mate matsie ("I have kept what I have seen."), 118
mathematics, 108
Mayo, Kevin, 64
mbongi (Kikongo institution), 118
McKeown, Greg, 166
McPherson, Satyani, 70*n*
mediation, 43
medicine and medical research
    Egyptian texts on, 108
    and fostering community resilience, 98
    Moore on changing nature of, 10, 185
    unethical experiments in, 10, 79–80, 193–94
meditation
    crystal bowl, 56, 60
    and music, 63
    notebooks for recording thoughts, 63
mental health services
    and confidentiality, 163, 169
    Jones on providing, 11, 156, 159, 160, 164, 167
    Jones on self-care and, 159, 165–67, 171–72
    surveys on, 171, 173
    and trauma-informed policies, 174
    for young men on color, 146, 151
mentoring/facilitation roles, 28
middle schoolers, 137, 163
mindfulness
    benefits of, 44
    Chatman's practice of, 49
    and eating, 59, 60
    and meditation, 44, 49, 56, 173, 177
    using social-cultural context for, 58–60
    and Wright, 50–51, 58–60

Mindfulness Integration for Nonviolent Development. *see* Project Youth Mind
miseducation of the negro, 119
Moore, Quinta
   on building trust and involvement, 191
   on changing traditional medical research, 10, 185
   as IRL alumna, 75
   on parachute research, 189
   on protecting people of color in research, 10, 187, 194
morning stretches, 64
Moscone Center, 143
"movin' on up," 108
music
   differences between Black and White, 125
   use of, in Project Youth MIND, 63, 64
   in Youth MIND, 64
music videos, 64
"My Identity is Community" (research collective), 140
My Ishmael (Quinn), 122

N

National Institutes of Health (NIH), 75, 78, 98
Neighborhood A (case study), 85–88, 90, 91, 93, 94, 97
Neighborhood B (case study), 85, 86–87, 88–90, 91, 93–97
New York State Department of Education, 125
Nobles, W. W., 121
nonprofits
   accessing opportunities, 135
   benefiting from research, 78
   in case study - Neighborhood A, 87, 94
   in case study - Neighborhood B, 88
   and work with EOBHC, 132–34
   and work with FCDI, 113
Nonviolent Communication, 64, 68
Norfolk State University, 42, 70*n*
notebooks, 63, 166
Nutricide: The Nutritional Destruction of the Black Race (Afrika), 120–21
Nyansa nnsa da (wisdom has no limits), 120–22

O

Oakland, California. *see* East Oakland Building Health Communities (EOBHC); East Oakland Youth Development Center (EOYDC)
observing *vs.* awareness, 59
Orisha (religion), 48
outcome, resilience as, 76

P

pandemic. *see* Covid-19 pandemic
parachute research, 189
parents
   consent from, 62
   and participation in CBPR projects, 8, 53, 62, 72
   and supporting stable parent-child relationships, 159, 168, 174
   surveys from, 169, 171, 173
participatory research. *see* community-based participatory research (CBPR)
peace circles, 43
Pedagogy of the Oppressed (Freire), 123
peer jealousy, 65
peer review, 195
Perry, Sparkle, 56, 70*n*
photography, 146
Pittsburgh. *see* Allegheny Co., Pittsburgh, PA
Pittsburgh, University of, 16

Pittsburgh Steelers, 32
poetry
  EOYDC project, 138, 140, 141–43
  in Project Youth MIND, 45, 190
Point Park University, 16
police
  abuse and violence by, 27, 37, 67, 80
  and founder of Gwen's Girls, 30
  and racial profiling, 57
  in schools, 37
polio vaccine, 79
"the Portrait Project," 148–50
posters, 143
power
  abuse of, 79–80, 104, 120
  decentralizing, 10
  to enhance resilience, 37, 45, 69, 77, 187
  imbalance in, in research, 5
  and participation, 189
  of research institutions, 75, 78
  sharing, 19, 21, 76, 80–85
  trust and diversity, 186–95
Power Point presentations, 64
probation officers, 64
problem behavior, 23
process, resilience as, 76
Project Youth MIND (PYM)
  Chatman as team member of, 9, 42, 48–50, 52–54, 59
  and dealing with racism and resilience, 45–46
  designing, 52–54
  and digital divide, 66–68
  effect of Covid-19 pandemic on, 9, 43, 47, 61
  employs ecological model, 42
  impact of, 68–72, 70n
  implemented as virtual program, 61
  importance of arts in, 43, 45, 60, 190
  pilot program 2020, 60–62
  and social emotional learning (SEL), 47
  Summer 2019 team, 70n
  testing program at DCDPR sites, 54–58, 61–64
  trivia game, 55
  use of arts in, 42, 43, 45, 60
  use of mindfulness in, 9, 42, 44, 54, 56
  Wright as team member of, 9, 42, 58–60, 70n
  youth engagement in, 62–66
promotion in academic research, 81, 195
prosocial behaviors, 94, 97
proverbs, 118
Pryce, Okevia, 70n
psychology
  Black, 10, 119, 124–25
  and community resilience, 76
Pythagoras, 108

Q
Quinn, Daniel, 122

R
racism
  effect upon Black youths, 45–46
  fatalities resulting from, 109–10
  racial profiling, 57
rap sessions, 64
recreation centers, 54–58, 61–64, 160
recruitment
  of girls for BGALA, 25–26
  for IRL research team, 42
  of participants for CBPR research, 71, 92, 158
  problems recruiting participants, 167, 176
  of professors and researchers, 79
  of research study participants, 191–92
  and trust, 32, 191
  use of flyers for, 168, 170, 173

relationships
  building, 89–90
  parent-child, 168
  strained, 80
religion and spirituality
  African, 48, 49, 109
  as coping mechanism, 139, 141
  differences between Black and White, 125
  faith-based organizations, 113, 160, 168, 186
research and researchers
  accountability to community and peers, 82, 85
  changing nature of medical research, 10, 185
  community trust in, 191–92
  decentralization of, as core principle of CBPR, 92
  decolonizing, 112–17
  defined, 75–76
  and development budget, 75, 78
  diversifying perspectives in, 193–94
  ethics in, 80–84
  impact of community partners and trust on, 90–92
  institutions and power sharing, 188
  parachute, 189
  poetry as component of, 138
  researchers may become part of community, 190
  salary coverage for, 81
  sharing with communities, 96
  timelines, 34, 138, 162, 170, 175, 178
  triggering memories, 146
  vetting researchers, 11, 136, 146, 152
  White women as, 33
resilience
  access to and control over resources, 78
  among Black youths, 45
  from an African-centered perspective, 103–4
  changing views on, 1
  community, and stigmatization by media, 89
  community, importance of, 76–77
  and culture of health, 159
  definitions and core concepts of, 1, 6, 158, 184
  dialogic model for, 126–27
  ecological nature of, 184–86
  importance of self-care in, 161, 171–73, 176–78, 186
  kits for use during pandemic, 61, 63
  multicultural interpretations of, 196
  outcomes for neighborhoods in case studies, 94–97
  and Portrait Project, 146–51
  for research team, 53
  theme of IRL cohort (2017), 22
  see also specific projects
restorative circles, 54, 55, 64–65
restorative justice practices
  to de-escalate and resolve conflicts, 66
  pillars of, 64
  in Project Youth MIND, 42, 43, 68
  workshops, 56
Richards, D. (Ari), 121
riddles, 118
risk
  ambiguity of, 6–7, 184
  and ecological factors, 185–86
  factors for Black youths, 45–46
  of harm to research participants, 4, 82–83
  of involvement in criminal justice system, 43–44

Robert Wood Johnson Foundation
(RWJF). Interdisciplinary Research
Leaders (IRL)
and allocation of grant dollars, 83–84
composition of cohort teams, 42
funds FCDI, 113
requirements and purpose of, 3, 83
value and recognition of CBPR, 98
see also specific projects
Rouse, Robert, 70*n*

S
Safe Routes to School, 140
safe spaces, 140–42
salary coverage, 81
sand timers, 63
San Francisco
Benioff Children's Hospital, 150
Joint Medical Program with UC
Berkeley, 145
Sarbeeb (communication system from
Somalia), 118
schools
closures, due to pandemics, 176
mindfulness programs in, 44
police-free, 37
recruitment flyers distributed in, 168, 170
restorative justice programs in, 43
safe routes to, 140–42
segregation in D. C., 66–68
suspension and expulsion from, 66
trauma-informed policies in, 174
underfunded, 45
violence in, 65
virtual schooling, 72
visits to, in designing Youth MIND, 52
science education, 108
scientific colonialism, 121
seed of culture *(Asili)*, 124

segregation, 66–68
self-care
impact of Covid-19 upon, 176–78
Jones on, 159, 165–67, 171–72, 192
and resilience, 161, 171–73, 176–78, 186
self-harm, 156
selfie sessions, 150
self-portrait photography, 146
self-reflection, 192
Seminerio, Caitlin, 70*n*
sex trafficking, 156
shame, 146
Shetgiri, R., 8
Shona (native language), 118
"shout-outs," 64
Smith, Patricia, 64
social capital, 144, 188
social distancing, 61, 72
social emotional learning (SEL), 47
socialization
and academic jargon, 188
at beginning of research project, 148
in violence prevention, 69
social justice
CBPR rooted in, 5
Chatman's interest in, 49
and Project Youth MIND, 42, 43
and spoken word sessions, 57
social media
for mindfulness, 60
as trigger for violence, 65
sociology, 76
soft skills, 92
Somalia, 118
Sonoma State University, 142
Sound Vibronics music meditation
sessions, 63
South Korea, 50
Spelman College, 134
spirit realm, 121

spirituality. *see* religion and spirituality
spoken word sessions
    favored by youth, 68
    Green as consultant for, 57, 64, 70*n*
    impact of racial disparity in COVID-19 upon, 67
    and social justice, 57
    as workshop in PYM 2019 session, 45, 54, 56, 60, 70
sports, 57
squad goals, 141
staff meetings, 65
STEM education, 114
stigmatization, 89–90
storytelling, 138
stress, 54
stress balls, 63
"Strong Parents, Stable Children" (curriculum), 168
Structured Dialogue method (SDM)
    African cultural basis of, 118–24
    as culturally responsive communication platform, 114–17
    and FCDI, 113
    Kheru on, 10, 196
Substance Use and Mental Health Services Administration, 171–72
suicide, 156, 164
summer camps, 61–62
surveys
    in BGALA evaluation, 26
    in Jones's research, 168, 169
    in Moore's research, 88, 92, 93, 95
    online, 171, 173
    in Project Youth MIND, 57, 68, 92, 93, 95
suspensions from school, 27, 43, 66
syphilis, 79

T
tabletop chimes, 63
tablets (computers), 67
Taylor, Breonna, 37, 47
team care, 177
TEDx talks, 64
Teenage Brain, 68
Teen Programs Office, 53–54
teleworking, 67
tenure, 81, 195
Tides Center, 113
timelines, 34, 138, 162, 170, 175, 178
Title IX, 17
transportation
    to BGALA, 25
    improved, for community residents, 93
    purchase of cars, 92
trap houses, 140
trap music, 60
trauma
    professionals' exposure to, 178–79
    racial, in education, 10, 108–12
    sessions in, for Project Youth MIND, 54
    and Triune brain model, 58
    types of, 156
Triune brain model and trauma, 58
trivia games, 67
Trump, Donald, 36–37
trust
    African Americans' lack of, in health care system, 80
    central to CBPR, 9
    establishing, between community and researchers, 88–92, 96
    power, and diversity, 186–95
    in research process, 191–92
"Tuskegee Study of Untreated Syphilis in the Negro Male," 79
Twi language, 120

Index

U

Understanding and Addressing Institutionalized Inequity: Disrupting Pathways to Juvenile Justice for Black Youth in Allegheny County (BGEA), 37
universities
  classroom presentations in, 144
  and historically Black colleges, 134
  power imbalances with community, 194
  as research institutions, 78
  success of university-based researchers, 194–95
  see also specific colleges and universities
U. S. Census zip code data, 66*n*

V

value neutral anti-bullying programs, 31
vans, 25
Vedic teaching, 56
vetting researchers, 11, 136, 146, 152
video conferences, 52
  see also Zoom
violence
  in communities and schools, 65
  and conflicts in social media, 65
  domestic, 156, 160
  EOYDC as coping mechanism, 140–42
  gang, 132
  by police, 27, 37, 67, 80
  prevention for Black girls, 22–23
  violence interrupters, 64
  Youth Violence Presentation Summit, 175
  youth violence prevention, 22, 62–69, 175
virtual schooling, 72
volunteering, 191

W

Washington, D.C. *see* District of Colombia; Project Youth MIND
Watson, Lilla, 33
web-based platforms, 168, 170, 174
webinars, 37, 175
wellness, 171–73, 177
White children *vs.* Black
  differences in learning, 125
  poverty statistics, 18
  protection from harassment and abuse, 23
  referrals to juvenile justice system, 17
White participants in research, 66–67, 110
White privilege, 36
Williams, Robert, 110
Wire, The (TV show), 63
wisdom has no limits *(Nyansa nnsa da)*, 120–22
word problems, 118
Wright, Ryan
  on arts and community, 190
  on collaboration, 186
  on entanglement with community, 192
  on involving young people in research, 196
  limitations of academic scholarships, 196
  and practice of mindfulness, 50–52
  on problematic nature of resilience, 184
  and Project Youth MIND, 9, 42, 58–60, 70*n*
  on siloed nature of academic fields, 188
  on time constrains in research, 195
  on trust and recruitment, 191

Y

yoga, 43, 54, 56, 58, 63, 70, 70*n*
Youth and Families in Crisis, 42, 70*n*

youth violence prevention
    as IRL cohort theme (2017), 22
    youth engagement in Project Youth MIND, 62–69
youth workers, 64
Y U Gotta Call It Ghetto? (poetry anthology), 142, 146

Z

Zip, Zap, Zoom (game), 55
zip code data, 66*n*
Zoom
    and digital divide, 66–68
    for family holiday "gatherings," 72
    for Gwen's Girls' meetings, 37
    for Project Youth MIND, 64